FIGHTING IRISH
MADNESS

Great Eras in Notre Dame Football

GOLDEN
OF COLLEGE SPORTS
AGES

FIGHTING IRISH MADNESS

Great Eras in Notre Dame Football

WILTON SHARPE

CUMBERLAND HOUSE
NASHVILLE, TENNESSEE

Fighting Irish Madness
Published by Cumberland House Publishing, Inc.
431 Harding Industrial Drive
Nashville, TN 37211–3160

Cover design: Gore Studio, Inc.
Text design: John Mitchell
Research assistance/data entry: Caroline Ross, Ariel Robinson

Library of Congress Cataloging-in-Publication Data

Sharpe, Wilton.
  Fighting Irish madness : great eras in Notre Dame football / Wilton Sharpe.
    p. cm.
  Includes bibliographical references and index.
  ISBN-13: 978-1-58182-518-3 (pbk. : alk. paper)
  ISBN-10: 1-58182-518-8 (pbk. : alk. paper)
  1. Notre Dame Fighting Irish (Football team)—History. 2. University of Notre Dame—Football—History. I. Title.
  GV958.N6S43 2006
  796.332'630977289—dc22

                                                              2006019339

Printed in the United States of America

1 2 3 4 5 6 7—12 11 10 09 08 07 06

For those two little leprechauns,
Xander and Gunner

and

for Caroline,
and the dream we dream

Ralph Guglielmi

CONTENTS

PREFACE

As a 10-year-old boy growing up in southern Connecticut, I remember being transfixed by the actions of a certain Notre Dame quarterback in the fall of 1954, presented before me on a movie theater screen via the old black-and-white Movietone newsreel that preceded a Saturday main feature matinee.

It was my initiation into the magical kingdom of Notre Dame football. What I witnessed was the wizard-like ball handling skills, agile running, and pinpoint passing of Ralph Guglielmi. Few would disagree that exposure to the 1954 consensus All-America QB was a fabulous way to be introduced to Golden Domedom. Oh yeah, it was still in the criss-cross-topped leather helmet days, when Domers wore the green *every* game, not just for special occasions. The Hornung era followed, and then a decade fairly flew by before that eagerly anticipated day in November 1966, when Michigan State and the Fighting

I t wasn't football as Notre Dame plays it today. It really was more like rugby. We'd bunch together and try to wedge the ball forward for the five yards needed for a first down.

Frank "Dutch" Fehr
member of the first Notre Dame team in 1887

A ccording to one historian, the victory over Army in 1913 was "the greatest single miracle in the history of Catholic higher education" because it began the transformation of Notre Dame "into a household word."

Murray Sperber
author

T he Notre Dame tradition was built on excellence. It consists of winning football games, developing quality young people, and responding to every situation with integrity.

Ty Willingham
head coach (2002–2004)

G us Dorais and Knute Rockne were the first players to see the real potential of the forward pass. Every day in the summer of 1913 the two worked on throwing the ball, and Dorais perfected a spiral delivery that could send the ball 30 and 40 yards downfield—phenomenal distances for the day.

Mike Celizic
author/sports columnist

I t is superior for ground-gaining purposes; it is less dangerous to the players, and it makes for a prettier game to view from the sidelines.

Anonymous newspaper account
*of the 1913 Notre Dame-Army game,
in which the Irish's use of the forward pass
became the talk of the nation*

I 'm not saying divine intervention helps us win football games. It's just that Notre Dame is a special place.

Lou Holtz
head coach (1986–96)

T he first time I came to campus after I was hired, they introduced me at halftime of a basketball game. The kids stood up and gave me a 15-minute ovation. A few weeks later, one of the dorms held an impromptu pep rally outside in 28-degree weather. There must have been hundreds of kids there all yelling like mad. I'd never seen anything like it. I'd heard about Notre Dame tradition, but I didn't know it could be like that.

Gerry Faust
head coach (1981–85)

E dward "Moose" Krause was one of the most beloved figures to operate under the Golden Dome, from the day in 1930 when Knute Rockne recruited him to play football for the Irish until his death in 1992. On the Notre Dame campus, it was harder to find a Moose detractor than an atheist.

Bob Logan
longtime Chicago Tribune *and* Daily Herald
writer/author,

John Heisler
Notre Dame Senior Associate
Athletic Director/longtime sports information
director/author,
on the 1932 second-team All-America tackle, star
hoopster, and 32-year Fighting Irish
athletic director

T hrough 2004, Notre Dame still had college football's most hallowed legacy. After 116 seasons, the Fighting Irish had only 12 losing seasons. Their 11 national championships, seven Heisman Trophy winners, and 78 consensus All-Americans are all collegiate bests.

Steve Delsohn
author/writer

There's little doubt that the 1930 era's two most popular teams were baseball's high-flying Yankees and football's unbeatable Fighting Irish, popular in that they were either the most loved or the most hated. And each team was led by the country's most dynamic personalities of the time—Babe Ruth and Knute Rockne.

Bill Cromartie
Jody H. Brown
authors

In 1942, Frank Leahy switched me to quarterback. He also went to the T, which was a monumental change for Notre Dame, because you're getting rid of the Rockne Shift. That was an honored piece of Notre Dame folklore.

Angelo Bertelli
tailback/quarterback (1941–43)

FAST FACT: *Bertelli threw for over 1,000 yards in his breakout sophomore season in 1941, finishing second in the Heisman Trophy balloting. Two years later, he became the first Notre Dame player to win the prestigious award*

N otre Dame is a special place. Players live in the dormitories with the rest of the students, preserving the tradition of Notre Dame football as an important part of campus life. Of course, winning is an essential part of that tradition.

Ty Willingham

T he four years, 1946–1949, have been dubbed "The Golden Era of Notre Dame Football."

Jack Connor
halfback-end (1948–49)/author,
on that unparalleled period in which Notre Dame
went unbeaten in 38 straight games, won three
national championships, spawned two Heisman
Trophy winners (Johnny Lujack, Leon Hart), two
Outland Trophy winners (George Connor, Bill Fis-
cher), eight future Hall of Famers (Lujack, Hart,
Connor,
Fischer, Emil "Red" Sitko, Ziggy Czarobski, Bob
Williams, and Jerry Groom),
and 12 All-Americans

THE GOLDEN YEARS

Many collegiate gridiron powers have experienced pinnacle success, but none compare to the performance of Notre Dame over the years. Beginning in 1913, when the Irish defeated Army in a stunning 35–13 upset on the plains of West Point, Notre Dame began its unparalleled surge to dominance in college football.

Nothing in college gridiron annals matches the awe-inspiring achievement of Knute Rockne's .881 winning percentage (105–12–5), ranked No. 1 all-time among both college and pro football coaches. The Rock also claimed three national championships during his 13-year tenure in South Bend (1924, 1929–30) and is still Notre Dame's all-time winningest coach. Not far behind is Frank Leahy's formidable .855, second all-time among college coaches, fashioned from an 87–11–9 worksheet. Leahy one-upped Rockne in national championships, garnering four (1943, 1946–47, 1949), including three in four years.

Notre Dame football would further leave its distinct winning mark on the decades of the 1960s, '70s, and '80s, notching national championships in 1966, 1973, 1977, and 1988 under three different mentors: Ara Parseghian, Dan Devine, and Lou Holtz. The school's eleven national titles rank No. 1 all-time in college football annals.

T owering above the northern goalposts, on the side of the 14-story Hesburgh Library, was the 132-foot-high mosaic of Christ. Since the mural, which was completed in 1964, depicted Christ with his arms extended upward, Notre Dame's students dubbed it Touchdown Jesus. By 1973, it was already college football's most famous image.

Steve Delsohn

A shaded statue of Father William Corby, an early Notre Dame president, depicts him as he gives mass absolution to Irish immigrant soldiers before the Battle of Gettysburg. Father Corby stands with one arm upraised. The students call him "Fair-catch Corby."

Roger Kahn
author/editor/writer

L ou Holtz continued the coaching tradition of winning a national championship in his third year at Notre Dame, just like Frank Leahy, Ara Parseghian, and Dan Devine.

Bob Logan
John Heisler

W herever I go, fans come up and remind me that the Irish are supposed to go 12–0—not just this year or next year, but every year.

Ty Willingham

T o attend a game at Notre Dame and to watch the medieval mania that settles upon the institution as game time approaches is to see football at its best

James Michener
renowned author,
from his Sports in America

THE BLUE
& GOLD

*T*ime and memory tend to be selective when the short list of so-called "greats" is called. Too often, the unnoted player with the heart of a warrior goes unrecognized, lost in the shadow of a Brady Quinn, a Jeff Samardzija, a Tim Brown, or a Joe Montana. Look deep into The Dame and you'll see the might that has earned the Fighting Irish its unparalleled niche in college football. Without them, the Blue & Gold could never have generated eleven consensus national championships and spawned seven Heisman Trophy winners, both tops in NCAA history.

H unk Anderson owns a most remarkable record for a lineman that still stands today. He is the only interior lineman in football history to score three touchdowns against one team, Purdue. Two of those historic tallies came within two minutes of each other in the 1921 game. Hunk blocked two Purdue punts, scooped up the ball each time, and battered into the end zone. The other touchdown of that classic football trilogy was an interception return of what appeared to be a Purdue screen pass for 32 yards.

Emil Klosinski
author/writer

MIGHTIEST OF THE MULES

The 1924 Fighting Irish, who brought the school its first-ever consensus national championship, will always be remembered for its immortal backfield of the Four Horsemen.

But no one knew better than the Horsemen what the men up front meant to their success. Though far less heralded than their backfield brethren, the Seven Mules were Notre Dame's equivalent to Fordham's famed Seven Blocks of Granite. And the main mule anchoring the heart of that line, the center and captain, was Adam Walsh.

He was the team's inspirational leader, a vicious tackler, and opportunistic blocker. No man played with greater courage. Walsh is canonized for his suck-it-up play against Army in '24, in which he played the entire game with two broken hands, yet never muffed a single snap in the famed Notre Dame box formation.

"On offense, he mastered all types of passes from center," author-writer-editor John D. McCallum noted in *We Remember Rockne*. "He had studied each of the Four Horsemen meticulously, knew what kind of hikes from center they each liked, and sensed just where to snap the ball."

L ou Rymkus, you're a battler.

Frank Leahy

head coach (1941–43, 1946–53),
on the rugged Irish tackle who required 12 stitches
in his mouth in a 20–0 win over Georgia Tech in
1941, after taking an elbow in the face. Rymkus's
wound re-opened twice during the game, but he
never left the field until just three minutes
remained

G eorge Ratterman was an incredible ball handler; he could fake the football with almost mesmeric skill. He was also a wonderful long passer—better than Lujack. His deft, spectacular talent led some Notre Dame fans to criticize Frank Leahy for not playing him more.

Bill Furlong

Sport magazine,
November 1965,
on the Irish QB from 1945 through '46

Z iggy was a better player than a lot of people gave him credit for. Because he was so funny and such a great personality it sort of overshadowed his ability, but he was good. He was a funny guy that kept everyone loose, but he was real serious during a game. He was one of those classic guys that wherever he went people would follow him around.

Creighton Miller
*halfback (1941–43)/backfield coach (1944),
on tackle Zygmont Pierre "Ziggy" Czarobski
(1942–43, 1946–47), voted into the College Football Hall of Fame in 1977 and one of the most
popular players ever to play
at Notre Dame*

B ob Kelly had an amazing year in 1944, in which he led the team in rushing (681 yards), receiving (283 yards), and in scoring (84 points, on 13 touchdowns and six PATs), putting him in a tie for second place among the nation's scorers. This was a Notre Dame record which would stand for 34 years until Vagas Ferguson surpassed it in 1979. Kelly also led the team in punt return average, kickoff return average, and kicked off until he hurt his leg. He came in sixth in the Heisman Award balloting and was named to several All-American teams.

Jack Connor
on the war years halfback (1943–44)

We were playing a game in about the middle of the season. Up to then, Elmer Angsman was an average halfback. In that particular game, he took the ball on a quick opener and lowered his shoulder on the linebacker. He popped that linebacker, bowled him right over, and kept on running for a touchdown. From that point on, it was like opening up a door, he just felt he could do this to everybody. He became one great halfback, and one of the nicest guys you ever want to meet. Of course, he eventually went on with the Chicago Cardinals as part of their "Dream Backfield."

Frank Tripucka
quarterback (1945–48)

All of Leahy's quarterbacks during the 1940s were excellent ball handlers, proficient in spins, reverse spins, and the art of deception. Frank Tripucka was the best—he was like a magician. Leahy used to proclaim that Tripucka was the best ball-handling, faking quarterback he ever had.

Jack Connor

In Frank Tripucka's only year as a starter, the senior completed 53 of 91 passes for 660 yards and 11 TDs. Tripucka, to Frank Leahy's delight, also threw no interceptions.

Steve Delsohn

Boley" Dancewicz was an excellent field general, a very good passer, and an outstanding defensive player. As a mark of his leadership, he was elected captain of the '45 team.

Jack Connor

T he name "Bob Williams" has no unique ring to it like "Marchy Schwartz" or "Bill Shakespeare," and he is by far the most anonymous of Notre Dame's Hall of Famers. He is often confused with the Bob Williams who quarterbacked the Irish in the late 1950s who was the architect of ND's monumental 7–0 victory over Oklahoma in 1957.

Jack Connor
on the 1949 consensus All-America
quarterback who guided the Irish to the national
championship that same year

J im Martin seemed bigger than life. He also represented the end of an era. He was in Notre Dame's last batch of servicemen.

Chet Ostrowski
end (1949–51)

J im Martin wouldn't hit you, he would kill you. Then he would smile and help you get back up.

Jack Connor
on the Irish end-tackle from 1946 through '49, who later logged 14 seasons in the NFL as a linebacker and placekicker

T ony Carey really had a great season for us. He led the nation [in 1964] with eight interceptions. And Tony was our hardest hitter. Pound for pound, Tony was the toughest football player I ever saw.

Ken Maglicic
guard (1962–64), on the 1964–65 Irish safety

G eorge Goeddeke was as tough as old work boots.

Mike Celizic
on the Irish center from 1964 through '66

George Goeddeke, from Detroit, grew up in a family of 12 children. He was the crazy kid, the one who claimed it was his duty to be wild because he had two brothers and two sisters in religious orders, and they needed someone to pray for.

Mike Celizic

By all accounts, Pete Duranko was the toughest man on that 1966 defensive front and the strongest man on the team.

Mike Celizic

If you want to see desire personified, look at Rocky Bleier.

Pete Duranko
defensive tackle (1964–66)

What kept him in the pros was that he could block your can off.

Tom Pagna
offensive backfield coach (1964–74),
on Rocky Bleier

I don't know if you want Tom sitting on the bench as a third-string quarterback or being named the number-one defensive back and probably being an All-American. It's your choice.

John Ray
defensive line coach/linebackers coach/
assistant head coach (1964–68),
to Tom Schoen's father before the start of
his son's junior season at ND. The father
reluctantly agreed to the position switch, allowing
Schoen, a standout high school quarterback, to
be moved to safety. Ray prophesied correctly:
Schoen intercepted seven passes in 1966—the
fourth highest number of picks ever recorded by a
Notre Dame player in a single season—and was
named a consensus All-American in 1967

L arry Conjar's customary devastating block-ing was a pastime he positively loved, because it gave him a chance to hit defensive ends and linebackers just as hard as they hit him when he had the ball. Conjar was six feet even and went around 215. An ideal fullback might have been a little bigger, but nobody played bigger

Mike Celizic
on the ND fullback of the mid-1960s

I f you talk about courage, Tom Rhoads had it. He was like what Mike Ditka calls the A.C.E.—great Attitude, great Character, and great Enthusiasm. You win with aces.

John Ray
*on defensive end Dusty Rhoads, part of the 1966
national championship team's
celebrated front four*

U ndefeated Pittsburgh jumped on us for a 17–7 lead [in 1978]. We didn't panic, however, and Joe Montana and Jerome Heavens brought us back for a 26–17 win. The game was significant for another reason— Heavens rushed for 120 yards on 30 carries to break George Gipp's all-time career rushing mark.

Dan Devine
*head coach (1975–80),
on the record-setting Irish fullback from
1975 through '78*

T he Gipper would have approved of this himself. You don't find a football player with more class than Jerome Heavens.

Joe Yonto
*defensive line coach (1964–80, 1986–87),
after Heavens broke Gipp's longtime school
career rushing mark (2,341 yards) set way back in
1920*

J oe Montana was not the only exceptional young man on that football team. There also was a player on the roster named Rudy Ruettiger, and anybody who has seen the movie *Rudy* knows all about him. . . . He now is a great inspirational speaker.

Dan Devine

in 2000, on the impassioned-but-undersized mid–
1970s scout team player who created
a legend at South Bend for his selfless,
dedicated play in practice

When I think about a tight end, I think of someone like Mark Bavaro. He's probably the strongest person I've ever worked with or been associated with. He's a gamer. Put that blue jersey on him and he's ready to go.

Gary Weil
onetime Irish strength coach,
on the Irish receiver from 1981 through '84

I don't think they could have nicknamed him better.

Gerry Faust
on Mark Bavaro's "Rambo" handle

He came to South Bend in 1993 with the sort of fanfare reserved for emperors or rock stars. ESPN analyst Beano Cook predicted Ron Powlus would win not one but two Heisman Trophies while leading the Irish to new heights. Powlus was helpless to protect himself against such hyperbole, so he wore that mission impossible around his neck like an albatross for the next five years.

Bob Logan
John Heisler

What I went through at Notre Dame taught me there's no situation I can't handle. I had some big games and we had winning teams, but it fell short of all those superlatives people expected of us. I walked away knowing I'll never quit, no matter how bad things get.

Ron Powlus
quarterback (1994–97)

kicker learns to have a short memory.

Jim Sanson
kicker (1996–99)

T ony Rice seldom piled up impressive statistics during his two and a half years (1987–89) as Notre Dame's starting quarterback. All he did was win. The youngster racked up a remarkable 28–3 record in games with him under center for the Irish. A rare blend of quickness, poise, and leadership enabled Rice to make lots of things happen at crunch time.

Bob Logan
John Heisler

The one thing about Tony Rice—he's as fine a competitor as I've ever been around. He's got the same kind of competitive attitude Steve Beuerlein had. Beuerlein could be bleeding, but he's going to fight you tooth and nail to win.

Pete Cordelli

receivers coach 1986–88)/
quarterbacks coach (1989–90),
on the quarterback of the 1988 national cham-
pion Fighting Irish. Beuerlein
quarterbacked Notre Dame from 1983 through
'86

Corny Southall is one of my favorite people of all time. He's a winner. He's a competitor. He's unselfish. I don't think we could have won it without him.

Lou Holtz

on the inspirational free safety from
1985 through '88

Anthony Johnson was one of the best full-backs I've been around, and this was on one ankle.

Lou Holtz
*on the tough Irish runner from 1986
through '89, who went on to star in the NFL for
11 seasons*

It's neat to get an encouraging phone call from Joe Montana during the week, but once we're in the huddle, it's time to forget the rah-rah stuff.

Rick Mirer
quarterback (1989–92)

Autry Denson ended up almost doubling the Gipper's 2,341 career rushing yards. In fact, once he started galloping, this dynamo didn't stop until he had surpassed the 4,131 yards churned out by Allen Pinkett from 1982–85.

Bob Logan
John Heisler

I'm an instinctive runner, but I learned to change pace and stay low, so tacklers couldn't slam into me. I take the hardest hits around the shoulders and keep driving with my legs.

Autry Denson
tailback (1995–97)/Notre Dame's all-time leader rusher, with 4,318 yards

In 2003, a human hurricane arose to blow away would-be tacklers and waft a fresh breeze of hope. That one-man offense turned out to be none other than Julius Jones, recycled, rededicated, and relentless.

Bob Logan
John Heisler

FAST FACT: Jones left school for a year in 2002, returning the following campaign to post one of the finest seasons in Notre Dame history, in which the talented tailback gained more than 200 yards in three separate games, including a school-record 262 yards against Pittsburgh, October 11, 2003.

Brady Quinn

When they were clicking in tandem, the Brady Quinn-Julius Jones dynamic duo sounded faint echoes of long-ago heroics by the likes of Bertelli-Miller, Lujack-Sitko, Hornung-Morse, Hanratty-Bleier, Montana-Ferguson, and Powlus-Denson.

Bob Logan
John Heisler

Brady's a level-headed guy. He knows the fans will measure him by how many games Notre Dame wins with him at quarterback. That matters to him a lot more than how many passes he completes.

Chinedum Ndukwe
safety (2003–2006),
on Brady Quinn,
who moved past Ron Powlus in 2005 as the lead-ing all-time passer in Notre Dame
history. Quinn also became the first ND passer to throw for more than 3,000 yards
in a season (2005)

They have more playmakers than anyone we've played. Jeff Samardzija is probably the best receiver we've played all year. They have more star power.

Kevin Simon

Tennessee linebacker,
after the Vols' 41–21 loss to the Irish in 2005.
Down 18 points, Tennessee fought back
to tie the game at 21 before bowing.
Samardzija's big late-third-quarter 73-yard pass
reception from Brady Quinn swung the momen-
tum back to ND. The go-ahead touchdown came
on a 4-yard aerial that Samardzija hauled in—
one of Quinn's three TD tosses on the day

J eff Samardzija increased his school-record single-season touchdown receptions mark to 15 and finished with nine catches for a career-high 216 yards to become Notre Dame's third career 1,000-yard single-season receiver.

Associated Press

after the last-minute 38–31 nail-biter over Stanford that closed out the 2005 regular season and 84-year-old Stanford Stadium. The Irish's All-America wideout pulled in two scoring aerials, including an 80-yarder, to help bring the Irish to a 9–2 record and a BCS bowl invitation in Charlie Weis's first year as head coach

ny high school quarterback would want to play for Coach Weis. There's something about him. He's from New Jersey, so he's got a little swagger to him. Kind of like me.

Jimmy Clausen
*Oaks Christian (Calif.) School senior
quarterback and the top recruiting prospect
in the nation for 2007, who has already
committed to Notre Dame*

rady Quinn enters his fourth season as a starter at Notre Dame and boasts an impressive blend of arm strength, size, and leadership skills. If his coverage reads and prudence continue to progress at a similar pace in 2006, Quinn could become the top pick in next year's draft.

Todd McShay
Scouts Inc.

Brady Quinn left normal behind about nine months and 32 touchdown passes ago, when he became a certified Golden Dome action hero by leading the resurgent Irish to a 9–3 season [in 2005]. When strangers recognize you on the beach in the Cayman Islands during spring break, normal is out the window. When fans are gathered outside your dorm at 7 a.m. the day of the spring game, forcing you out a side entrance to get to your car, normal is history.

Pat Forde
senior writer, ESPN.com

C ombine the elements—Notre Dame QB and Heisman Trophy front-runner on a preseason top-five team, playing for the ultimate offensive coach and possessing every imaginable off-the-field attribute—and you have Category 5 hype.

Pat Forde

on the publicity whirl surrounding Irish senior quarterback Brady Quinn for 2006

I t's hard to really even think about yourself [as a celebrity], or even to be labeled as a role model. I'm just a "slappy," as Coach Weis would say. Just a college student at Notre Dame, playing football, trying to have fun with it.

Brady Quinn

quarterback (2003–06)

IRISH CHARACTER

I've got to go, Rock. It's all right. I'm not afraid. Sometime, Rock, when the team is up against it, when things are wrong and the breaks are beating the boys—tell them to go in there with all they've got and win one for the Gipper. I don't know where I'll be then, Rock. But I'll know about it, and I'll be happy.

George Gipp
his famous deathbed request to Knute Rockne

I t's like you've played flag football all your life and for the first time you put on pads and go into combat. It's a big test of courage.

Bob Gladieux
halfback (1966–68),
a surprise starter in the titanic clash between No.
1 Notre Dame and No. 2 Michigan State in
1966, when regular halfback, All-American Nick
Eddy, was sidelined with a previously sustained
shoulder injury

D on't take yourself too seriously. It can't be a game for the players if it's not a game for you.

Dan Devine
his advice to coaches

M ost of my life I was a failure, or so I was told. I stopped listening to people tell me I couldn't make it.

Dan "Rudy" Ruettiger
defensive end (1975)

I saw him limping down the hallway. As a young man and a player, he had all the right qualities. Yes, he was one of my favorite players. And I thought it was admirable that he was going to give football a try again. But I wondered to myself, "Good lord, how is he ever going to do it?"

Ara Parseghian
on Rocky Bleier,
upon the 1967 Irish captain's return to Notre
Dame after serving in Vietnam. Bleier
sustained combat injuries that included a
bullet wound to his left thigh and a right foot
blown open by a grenade. Against all odds, Bleier
went on to an 11-year career with
the NFL's Pittsburgh Steelers, winning four Super
Bowl rings

I don't think about all the touchdowns or all the records. I think about what Notre Dame means and what it stands for and I try to live that.

Vagas Ferguson
*running back (1976–79),
onetime top career rusher (3,472 yards)
at Notre Dame and still holder of the
single-season rushing mark of 1,437 yards,
set in 1979*

My goal in life is not to see how much newsprint I can get. When people use football to gain popularity, it is very distressing to me.

Rusty Lisch
quarterback (1976–77, '79)

He plays with pain better than any football player I've seen in my 37 years of coaching.

Gerry Faust
on tight end Mark Bavaro

All opponents regard playing Notre Dame as their big game. I regard that as part of the experience that will help our young men to prepare for success in whatever they do later.

Lou Holtz

There's a difference between confidence and cockiness.

Pat Terrell
free safety (1986–89)

I just couldn't get used to that damn thing. In fact, when we played the Navy in 1941, I didn't have a facemask and they broke my nose. When I reached up to feel it, my nose was way over here. Under my eye. I kept playing of course. We all did at Notre Dame. With Leahy, you weren't hurt unless a bone stuck out.

Bob Dove
*end (1940–42)/two-time consensus
All-America*

The game is special for halfback Elmer Angsman's iron-man performance. He would end up losing nine teeth, and his lacerated mouth required 26 stitches. Still, after getting injured *in the first quarter*, Angsman played 54 minutes against Navy.

Steve Delsohn

on the physical 6–6 tie with Navy in 1945. Angsman would go on to play seven seasons with the NFL's Chicago Cardinals

Jim Martin did things that other people don't. Even in the Marines, how many guys had the nerve to swim beneath enemy ships and try to blow them up?

Jim Mutscheller

*end (1949–51),
on the Irish's WWII-hardened end-tackle,
a reconnaissance swimmer during the war*

Players in the 1940s and 1950s had a lot of intestinal fortitude. We had a lot of desire to excel. We were dedicated to our teams.

Jerry Groom
linebacker (1948–50)

What meant the most to me was our second-half attitude against USC. We were down 37–20 [in the fourth quarter], and our sideline was still intense. That's when we became a football team.

Lou Holtz
on the 1986 Irish team's remarkable winning effort against Southern Cal, coming from behind to win 38–37 in the final seconds

We play for 60 minutes. We've got the talent on this team, but it's more than that.

Jeff Samardzija
*wide receiver (2003–06),
on the heart of the 2005 Fighting Irish*

Against many obstacles and at the price of a long and tough rehabilitation program, Scott Zettek has managed to come back from not just one but two knee injuries!

Mike Shields

author,
on the Irish defensive end's inspirational play in
the 7–0 blanking of Alabama in 1980,
the Crimson Tide's first shutout loss on their
home field in 22 years. Zettek logged nine tackles
that afternoon and recovered
an Alabama fumble at the Tide 4-yard line
to set up the game's lone score

I came here with dreams of winning a national championship. Why would I ever go somewhere else, when this is my last chance?

Brady Quinn

on his decision to return for his senior season

IRISH
HUMOR

Most of Paul Hornung's correspondence could be divided into three categories: Redheads, blondes, and brunettes.

Dick Schaap
noted sports journalist
sports-talk TV host

Nothing is better than God.
Warm beer is better than nothing.
Therefore, warm beer is better than God.

Anonymous
carved into desktop at Notre Dame, 1966

God is dead.

— *Kierkegaard*

Kierkegaard is dead.

— *God*

Graffiti
scrawled on a Notre Dame classroom desktop

When he stood up and moved forward, the ocean of screaming, sweating students roared like a hurricane and chanted his name: "Ar-a! Ar-a!" Parseghian stood there with his arms raised and took it in, and as he did, he could never help thinking: "This is how Hitler got started."

Mike Celizic
on a pep rally preceding the 1966 season opener against Purdue

One time in practice a play was called for the first count. I thought it was on the second. A coach came running in yelling, "Why didn't you snap it?" I just told him I didn't want to part with the ball.

Dave Huffman
center (1975–78)

Don't bother, it was probably my father.

Rusty Lisch
*to a teammate who wanted to go after a fan
yelling insults about Lisch's quarterbacking*

I don't like reporters because I don't like seeing what I say in the papers.

Mark Bavaro
tight end (1981–84)

Lads, I want to tell you about this Illinois team. We fit about eight players on a bench. They are so huge, they only fit four on a bench. They have a middle linebacker by the name of Lester Bingaman. I had him to dinner in my Long Beach, Indiana, home. Lads, I have eight children. Four of them went away from the table hungry.

Frank Leahy

It was only right for Beth (Mrs. Lou Holtz) to buy cemetery plots for us close to the Lady on the Dome. The alumni used to bury me here every Saturday.

Lou Holtz

I see where *Sports Illustrated* listed us in their top 20. They could get more credibility by using a picture of me in their swimsuit issue.

Lou Holtz

I'd rather have a slow guy going in the right direction than a fast guy going in the wrong direction.

Lou Holtz

We have a lot of confidence in Reggie, especially from five yards in.

Lou Holtz
quipping on placekicker Reggie Ho

FAST FACT: Ho, the 135-pound Hawaiian walk-on never known for his lengthy kicks, was on his game against Michigan in 1988—the Irish's last national championship season—when he booted four field goals to help topple Michigan, 19–17.

Gipp was a man, Father O'Donnell once noted, who could sit in his English class and get 100 percent—50 from the student on his left and 50 from the student on his right.

Ray Robinson
author

Red Smith later wondered—since Grantland Rice had been in the upstairs press box at the Polo Grounds—"At what angle had he watched the game to see the Notre Dame backfield outlined against the sky?"

Murray Sperber
*on the famed sportswriter's pondering of Rice's
legendary newspaper lead that launched the Four
Horsemen. The story began, "Outlined against a
blue, gray
October sky, the Four Horsemen rode again."*

H e had that special ability to mobilize the whole gang of us through humor, laughter, jokes, songs, and, yes, even prayers. Who can forget Ziggy Czarobski yelling in the midst of a football game when things were not going right—"For chrissake, let's get back in the huddle and say a Hail Mary!"

Jim Mello
fullback (1942–43, '46)

Y ou show me a teammate with a straight-A average and I'll show you a guy that's letting his team down.

Ziggy Czarobski
tackle (1942–43, 1946–47)

T he Notre Dame defense saved us more times than Roy Rogers and Trigger had rescued the heroine.

Lou Holtz

Rockne had a habit of giving his players impromptu quizzes and once collared Frank Carideo's substitute in practice. "It's our ball on the enemy's 2-yard line, fourth down, goal to go," Rockne barked at the unsung quarterback. "What would you do?"

"Move over on the bench a little so I could see the touchdown better," replied the sub.

Paul Castner
halfback/fullback (1920–22)/author-writer

Maybe we'll try cutting some top rows out of the stadium to get a clear view of Touchdown Jesus. It would help us to have opponents see that.

Ty Willingham

Better me than Johnny Lattner.

Florence Leahy
Frank Leahy's wife,
to her husband, after she fell in their home
in 1953 and broke her leg

IRISH
LEGENDS

T he Four Horsemen were famed for their great speed and fast starts. They made their greatest gains off tackle or wider, as the backs did not have the weight for consistently bulling it up the center. All were great in every way, not the least of their greatness being that they starred as a team rather than as individual performers, although any one of them would have been an individual star in any backfield in the country.

Tim Lowery
Northwestern center (1924),
on the immortal backfield of right halfback
Don Miller, left halfback Jim Crowley, fullback
Elmer Layden, and quarterback Harry Stuhldreher

Rockne's single most fabled player was George Gipp. An extraordinary halfback and a prodigious gambler and drinker, he was named Notre Dame's first All-American in 1920. Gipp died at age 25 from a strep throat infection.

Steve Delsohn

George Gipp's season achievements in 1920 earned him consensus All-American honors—the first across-the-board All American at Notre Dame—and the plaudits of such eastern sportswriters as Grantland Rice.

Murray Sperber

He was a perfect performer who comes along only once in a generation.

Knute Rockne
*end (1910–13)/assistant coach (1914–17)/head coach (1918–30),
on George Gipp*

T his man Gipp is All-American or there is
no real All-American eleven this fall. If
anything can be done on a football field that
Gipp didn't do at West Point it isn't dis-
cernible to the naked eye. Notre Dame had
two teams on the field—Gipp and ten other
men. The Army couldn't stop Gipp no matter
what they did. He was a Titan on attack and a
concrete wall on defense.

New York Herald
November 1, 1920

T he strangest aspect of the brief, curious
career of George Gipp is that to this day
many people believe he was one of Notre
Dame's famous Four Horsemen.

Ray Robinson

George Gipp

The lean-muscled, 185-pound, six-foot Gipp, 21 and full of hell, immediately put his imprint on a freshman contest with Western State Normal of Kalamazoo, Michigan, October 7, 1916. With the score tied at 7–7 in the last quarter, Notre Dame had several yards to go on fourth down. . . . Operating out of punt formation, Gipp unexpectedly unleashed a booming 62-yard dropkick for a field goal. Western State's players were flabbergasted to lose a game in such a way.

Ray Robinson

George Gipp was the greatest player that Notre Dame ever produced . . . he was Nature's Pet . . . he had the timing of a tiger in pouncing on his prey . . . he was a master of defense . . . not a single forward pass was ever completed in territory that he defended.

Knute Rockne

H e could run from any point on the field, combining speed and power with a hip twist that made him the most dangerous man I ever saw in action. His play was a treat for technical connoisseurs of that time. His magnetic leadership, his genius as an open-field runner, his spine-tingling dashes and his matchless morale endeared him to thousands and made football history.

Heartley "Hunk" Anderson
*guard (1918–21)/assistant coach (1924–27,
1930)/head coach (1931–33),
on the immortal George Gipp*

F ollowing the classic contest at West Point [in 1920], they called him Lochinvar of the West, and held him a demi-god of Football.

The Dome
*1921 Notre Dame yearbook,
eulogizing George Gipp*

CREATING THE FOUR HORSEMEN

One of the great sports public relations-marketing success stories of all time unwittingly came about through the efforts of a nationally known sports journalist, a fabulously integrated backfield for a well-known winning team, and a little-known school publicist who put it all together.

The occasion of a visit to New York in October 1924 by one of Knute Rockne's first great Notre Dame teams to play an equally well-matched Army team at the Polo Grounds provided the setting. It took a fine performance on the field from four relatively unknown lads in the Fighting Irish backfield and one wondrously prosaic writer to capture their feats in sterling literary fashion that afternoon. But mostly it took an inventive Notre Dame student press assistant named George Strickler to put it all together.

It was Strickler who arranged the famous photo of the four backs on horseback and coupled it with Grantland Rice's timeless lead. Strickler then managed to get his package carried on the nation-wide wire services, and the legend of the Four Horsemen was launched.

O utlined against a blue, gray October sky, the Four Horsemen rode again. In dramatic lore, they are known as Famine, Pestilence, Destruction and Death. These are only aliases. Their real names are Stuhldreher, Miller, Crowley, and Layden. They formed the crest of the South Bend cyclone before which another fighting Army team was swept over the precipice at the Polo Grounds this afternoon as 55,000 spectators peered down upon the bewildering panorama spread out upon the green plain below.

Grantland Rice
renowned sports journalist,
his legendary lead in the New York
Herald-Tribune *the day following Notre Dame's*
13–7 victory over Army in 1924.
The classic piece launched immortality for the
four Irish backs and became a treasured icon of
sports journalism

The legendary Four Horsemen, from left, Jim Crowley, Elmer Layden, Don Miller, and Harry Stuhldreher

E ven by 1924 standards, we were small. By today's standards, we were almost midgets. We'd probably have trouble getting on most of today's college teams as student managers.

Elmer Layden
*fullback (1922–24)/head coach (1934–40)/ one of
the famed Four Horsemen,
in 1969*

J im Crowley was a left halfback whom Rockne considered one of the most versatile players he had ever coached or seen, because he could block and tackle as well as run and pass. If he had come along later in life, his physical talent, mental poise, and competitive flame would have made him a T-formation quarterback who just might have made Johnny Unitas move over a little.

Tim Cohane
*author/former sports editor, Look magazine,
on the Four Horsemen's left halfback*

O nce in the open field, Don Miller was the most dangerous of the Four Horsemen. He was the greatest open field runner I ever had.

Knute Rockne

on the right halfback and ball-carrying workhorse of the Four Horsemen, who averaged 6.8 yards a carry in his three years in South Bend

A n accident of Blasco Ibáñez's best-selling popularity inspired their name; by accident they were brought together. But it was no accident that made them collectively and individually fine players. That was design and hard work. The Four Horsemen have the right to ride with the gridiron great.

Allison Danzig

author/historian

Elmer Layden was the quiet member of the Four Horsemen and their star on defense. His ability to intercept passes was uncanny. He turned two interceptions into touchdowns for a big 27–10 victory over Stanford in the 1925 Rose Bowl game.

John D. McCallum
author/writer/editor

Without the Seven Mules to kick up the dust, our backfield would have bogged down. It was only through the great work of our linemen that the four of us did anything worth mentioning.

Harry Stuhldreher
quarterback (1922–24),
on Notre Dame's offensive line of that time,
known as the Seven Mules

I asked Rock who was the gamest man he ever coached at Notre Dame. His answer: "All Notre Dame men are game, dead game. The star example is Adam Walsh, who played brilliantly at center against a strong Army team although he had five broken bones in his two hands. He never made a bad pass. I didn't think Walsh could last 10 minutes, but he lasted 60 minutes."

Grantland Rice

Carideo, Brill, Savoldi, and Schwartz were a combination of four antelopes, four charging buffaloes, four digdigs, and four eels.

Grantland Rice
on the backfield of the 1929 and '30 national championship teams, satirizing his own earlier immortalization of the Four Horsemen

O n *Street & Smith's* All-Time Dream Team, which covered players from the first 50 years of its publication (1941–90), Bob Dove was chosen at defensive end on the second team, ranked behind Ted Hendricks of Miami and Hugh Green of Pittsburgh and alongside Bubba Smith of Michigan State.

University of Notre Dame
Official Athletic Site

B ob Dove was a hitter. He was exactly the kind of player Leahy wanted. That's why Leahy had so much live contact at practice. He wanted the hitters, not the hittees.

Bob McBride
guard (1941–42, '46)/line coach (1949–53)

My father was a starting halfback at Notre Dame in 1907, '08, and '09. My uncle Walter was the starting fullback with George Gipp. My uncle Don was one of the Four Horsemen. So when it came time to go to college, my father didn't ask me what college I wanted to attend. He told me what time the train left for South Bend.

Creighton Miller

Creighton Miller was one of the best runners I have ever seen. He had the quickest start—he would just burst in there.

Angelo Bertelli

FAST FACT: Miller led the nation in rushing in 1943 with 911 yards and topped Notre Dame in scoring, with 13 touchdowns. He posted the team's best kickoff and punt return averages and also led the Irish with six interceptions, finishing fourth in the '43 Heisman voting.

Creighty is the finest running back I ever played with, college or pro. I have not seen anybody that I thought could measure up to Creighton Miller. He could run the hundred in about 9.6 seconds. Keep in mind this is back in 1943. He weighed 195 pounds and might have been the trickiest back. Creighty could head-fake you and hip-fake you. He had bow legs and it just seemed like legs were coming at you from all directions—then suddenly he would dart past you. A pass catcher? He had the softest hands—anything that was near him he had.

Johnny Lujack
quarterback (1943, 1946–47)/
Heisman Trophy winner (1947)

Kevin Hardy, an enormous man with uncommon quickness and agility, was the last man in the history of Notre Dame to letter in football, basketball, and baseball.

Mike Celizic

There wasn't anybody going to get by me.

Kevin Hardy
defensive tackle (1964–67),
often criticized by ND assistant coaches
—who couldn't argue with his results—
that he wasn't mean enough

We just had no idea Seymour had that much speed. It was just impossible for us to stop him no matter what we tried. It was not a case of trying to adjust. He was just too much for us to handle. I don't think any pro defense could have stopped him either.

Jack Mollenkopf
former Purdue head coach,
following the Boilermakers' 26–14 loss to Notre
Dame in 1966, when the Irish unveiled their new
super-sophomore passing tandem of split end Jim
Seymour and quarterback Terry Hanratty. In that
game, Seymour caught 13 passes for 276 yards—
both Notre Dame single-game records—and
three
touchdowns. The yardage figure was the
second highest ever by a receiver in
NCAA history

This boy is the best pro prospect I've ever seen at any position. I believe he could make any professional team in the country right now.

Don Klosterman
*former Houston Oilers GM,
on standout receiver Jim Seymour,
then just four weeks into his sophomore year at
South Bend*

Nick Eddy's second kickoff return for a touchdown that year, against Pitt, had tied a school record. Amazingly, it had been only his fourth kickoff return of 1966 and gave him an average of 48.3 yards per return, a number unsurpassed by Heisman Trophy winners Paul Hornung and Tim Brown, and All-American wonder Rocket Ismail.

Mike Celizic

lan Page, at 6–5 and 240 pounds, was quick and strong and terrifying. Another All-American, he later became the first defensive player ever to be named the National Football League's most valuable player. His 15 years of excellence in the pros eventually earned him a bronze bust in the Pro Football Hall of Fame in his hometown of Canton, Ohio.

Mike Celizic

en MacAfee, a three-time All American, entered the College Football Hall of Fame in 1997. He is arguably the best tight end in the history of Notre Dame football.

Steve Delsohn
*on the two-time consensus All-America
tight end of 1976–77*

I didn't know him personally, but I've heard that George Gipp was a great individual as well as a great football player.

Jerome Heavens
fullback (1975–78),
after breaking Gipp's 58-year career rushing mark
in 1978

Tim Brown became Notre Dame's first Heisman Trophy winner since John Huarte in 1964. Brown finished his career in 1987 as the Irish's all-time leader in pass reception yards (2,493), kick-off return yards (1,613), and kicks returned for touchdowns (three punts, three kickoffs).

Steve Delsohn

After Tim Brown left [in 1987], everybody said, "There won't be another Tim Brown." Rocket wasn't ready as a freshman to be another Tim Brown. But now Rocket was a sophomore, and we felt Rocket was really going to be something special.

Lou Holtz
on speedy Raghib Ismail in 1989

I got finesse, but I don't use it much.

Jerome Bettis
fullback (1990–92)

I punish [opponents] when I need to. When Walter Payton got pursued to the sidelines, he never tried to run out of bounds. That's the way I want to play.

Jerome Bettis

LEGENDARY COACHES

He was a builder of spirit, the finest spirit the gridiron has ever known.

John Kieran
New York Times *columnist,*
on Knute Rockne

H is popularity is in its infancy.

The Dome
*1918,
on young first-year head coach Knute Rockne, an
assistant under Jesse Harper since 1914*

⁓

T here are only two excuses for missing practice: the death of one of your parents, or your own death.

Knute Rockne

⁓

Y ou don't have to see a good tackle, you can hear it.

Knute Rockne

⁓

K nute Rockne is loved and cherished here as much as he was in 1929 or 1930, when he had his unbeaten teams. His name is still magic.

Lou Holtz
1989

ockne's head coaching career at Notre Dame spanned 13 seasons (1918–1930) and 122 games. His team put a fabulous 105–12–5 record in the books, and his .881 winning percentage is *still* the highest of any coach at the college and pro football levels. What makes his record even more glowing is that he played top teams from all sections of the country—most away from home. Rockne's 13-year schedule called for only 48 games at South Bend and 74 on the road.

Bill Cromartie
Jody H. Brown

balding, broken-nosed genius, Knute Rockne did more than win a school-record 105 games. He transformed a small and obscure Catholic university into an American institution.

Steve Delsohn

G ive them hands and knees and elbows! Give 'em everything but abuse!

Knute Rockne
to his linemen

I have been asked innumerable times—had Rockne lived, what role would he have played in modern football? My answer is always the same: Rockne would still be the leader. He had developed his mind to such a degree that he was always far ahead of his contemporaries—and I have no reason to believe that these last 43 years would have changed him. He was a great analyst, a deep thinker, and he was one who could adjust to given situations.

Frank Carideo
quarterback/punter/punt returner (1928–30)

UNIVERSITY OF NOTRE DAME

Knute Rockne

O ne reason Rockne was so successful was his intelligence. He probably would have been a great success in any other line of work he might have chosen. . . . As a coach, he knew how to motivate his players, and that's a key to long-range success in sports.

Lou Holtz

T he toughest poison a coach has to face in football is over-confidence. This can wreck any team. That's why coaches rarely predict a victory, even when they expect to win hands down. . . . You either put out all you have, or you get put out.

Knute Rockne

S how them your scrapbooks. They don't know how good you are.

Knute Rockne
to one of his Irish teams losing at halftime

T he only qualifications for a lineman are to be big and dumb. But to be a back, you only have to be dumb.

Knute Rockne
chewing out his squad at practice

G o on out there and hit 'em, crack 'em, crack 'em, smack 'em! Fight to live. Fight to *win, win, win, win!*" In the years to come, generations of moviegoers would hear this staccato style mimicked by veteran actors such as Pat O'Brien and J. Farrell MacDonald, performing as Rockne in their maudlin worst.

Ray Robinson

Rockne regarded football as drama and the squad as a cast. In essence he tried to make a theater out of both the practice field and the stadium, to keep both spectators and participants entertained at all times.

Edwin Pope
longtime Miami Herald *sports columnist*

Rockne wanted to win more than he wanted to live.

Francis Wallace
author/historian and onetime
ND student press agent,
on Frank Leahy

oose Krause was one of the few threads left to all of the glory days. He'd practiced with Rockne's varsity squad and coached under Leahy. As athletic director, he'd hired Parseghian, and in the mid-eighties, although retired, he'd advised the administration to make Holtz the head man. By then he'd become the athletic director emeritus at Notre Dame. "That means that I still work but I don't get paid for it," he often told people. . . . At 79, he remained very involved.

Stephen Singular
author/writer

Frank Leahy was a slew of contradictions. He dressed expensively in double-breasted dark suits, wide-brim hats, and bow ties. But Leahy worked such late hours that he often slept on campus and wore the same rumpled clothes for days at a time.

Steve Delsohn

When you came back to Notre Dame after the summer, Leahy would look at your hands. If they weren't covered with calluses, Leahy figured you were a candy ass.

Creighton Miller

Prayers work better when the players are big.

Frank Leahy
TIME *magazine, October 11, 1946*

Frank Leahy was the best coach I ever player for.

George Connor
*tackle (1946–47)/two-time consensus
All-American (1946–47)*

S ometimes he got so excited during the pep talks, he foamed at the mouth.

Jim Mello
on Frank Leahy

I think that he tried to pass on to his boys the message from his coach (Rockne) and his father—that life was real and earnest; that one got what one earned and fought to hold; that the game of life, like the football field, was no place for a coward or a weakling; and damned be he who first cried *Hold. Enough.*

Francis Wallace

L eahy was a great coach right after World War II. He was dealing with men. War veterans. Leahy could work the shit out of them. And they could handle that pressure. But all the war vets were gone by 1950. The younger players had different temperaments. And Leahy ruined a lot of those young guys. They couldn't take the pressure he put on.

Chet Ostrowski

F rank Leahy was fired. But I'm not going to put in print why he was fired. Forty years ago, I promised Father [Theodore] Hesburgh I wouldn't do that. And I intend to keep that promise to him.

Terry Brennan
halfback (1945–48)/head coach (1954–58)

Y ou know why Notre Dame is the best college team in the country? It's because
Frank Leahy is the greatest college football
coach who ever lived. He's greater than Knute
Rockne ever thought of being and I'm not
knocking old Rock. But Leahy is just the best.
. . . They complain and say that he teaches
dirty football and all that silly talk. The reason
they complain is that Leahy is superior and he
wins. They stay clear of Notre Dame for one
reason: Frank Leahy. They don't want to get
beat.

Red Grange

R ockne could beat them and make them
like it. Leahy beats them and they wind up
hating his guts.

Francis Wallace

eahy always dressed well. He wore a dark suit, a bow tie, and a large hat. We called it a "hood" hat, because it had the wide brim like the hoods in Chicago wore. Leahy was always famous for stomping on his hat. One time he took the hat and flung it out onto the field. But it was so blustery, the hat turned around and came back just like a boomerang. It hit Leahy right in the head. He looked down and said, "Where did that thing come from?"

Jack Lee
guard (1951–54)

rank Leahy had the ability to get more out of an athlete. He would convince folks to do far beyond what they thought they were capable of doing.

Jack Connor

As many tough guys as there were around here, I always thought that Leahy was tougher than any of them. Physically and mentally, you take the toughest guy on our team, and Leahy was tougher.

Creighton Miller

This use of "gents and lads" by Leahy was something the players had to get accustomed to. Leahy had a very distinct way of speaking which sounded very formal. When talking to or about one of his players, he used the player's full name instead of the commonly used nickname.

Jack Connor

Vince Lombardi told me Frank Leahy was the single most important influence on his life in football. (Lombardi was one of the Seven Blocks of Granite at Fordham—Leahy was his line coach.) He said everything he knew—all the basics, the philosophy, all the intricate parts of football—he learned from Leahy.

Jerry Groom

I only played for two coaches in college and in pro ball, Frank Leahy and George Halas. I think Leahy was 10 times better than Halas. Leahy had it over everybody as a preparatory coach, as a fundamentals coach, as a motivator, and as an innovator. I thought Leahy was the all-time greatest coach who ever came down the pike.

Johnny Lujack

They fired Terry Brennan at the wrong time. He was a better coach when they fired him than when they hired him. Terry wasn't ready when they hired him [in 1954]. By the end of 1958, he was a seasoned coach who'd been through some stuff. He had all the scars you'd want.

Ed Mieszkowski

tackle (1943–45)

I enjoyed being coach at Notre Dame. We were a Top Ten team three years out of five. We played some pretty good football. Sure, there were frustrations. But who said life is fair?

Terry Brennan

J oe Kuharich was a disciplinarian. He believed in working you to death. He kept saying that first spring [of 1959]: "We don't know how far we can push these bodies."

Ken Adamson
guard (1957–59)

K uharich was a meathead. I played for him in the pros. He was head coach when I was with the Cardinals. Do you know we never had a screen play in our whole repertoire? I can't tell you what a hardheaded Croatian that guy was.

Bill Fischer
tackle (1945–48)

J oe Kuharich was certainly an unfortunate selection. He was the image of the belea-guered football coach. As he would explain defeats with his long-suffering demeanor, he seemed willing to go on forever being 5–5.

John Underwood
Sports Illustrated *writer*

Brennan had been no Leahy and Kuharich was no Brennan.

Steve Delsohn

In 1964, Ara came in and lit the place up. But Kuharich had no emotion. His teams had no emotion. It was like playing behind the Iron Curtain.

Ed Burke
tackle (1960–62)

Ara Parseghian, who made the College Football Hall of Fame in 1980, left Notre Dame with a 95–17–4 record. In 1964, he took over a woebegone program and returned it instantly to national prominence. Parseghian won two national championships. His 1973 team went 11–0, Notre Dame's first perfect year since 1949. There were victories in the Cotton, Sugar, and Orange bowls, all of them over No. 1-ranked teams.

Steve Delsohn

A ra Parseghian's stature on campus rivaled that of the golden dome.
Mike Celizic

N otre Dame wants its coaches to be like its priests. They have to be able to enjoy a drink without getting drunk and enjoy the company of women without fooling around.
Jim Lynch
linebacker (1964–66, captain '66)

I t was just meeting Ara. He was as honest as any man could be.
Terry Hanratty
quarterback (1966–68),
on why he went to Notre Dame

Y ou couldn't play for a better man than Ara Parseghian.
Bump Elliott
former Michigan coach,
to ND recruit Jim Seymour, after losing his bid to
land the highly sought-after prospect from
Berkley, Michigan

He never let up. He always had that intensity. All good coaches have the fear that everything is going to go wrong. Every pass is going to be intercepted. There'll be a fumble on every play. Every call will go against them.

Joe Doyle
South Bend Tribune *sports editor emeritus,*
on Ara Parseghian

By all accounts it was nearly impossible to find another football coach as organized and with as fine an eye for detail as Ara Parseghian. It was the reason for his success. He didn't do things because he thought they might work but because he was convinced they would work.

Mike Celizic

Anyone who would get into coaching is nuts.

Ara Parseghian

W hen motivating a team, *where* you say it is as important as *what* you say.

Dan Devine

O n my way up, loyalty and hard work were high priorities. Emotions, preparations, and discipline are all important factors in playing winning football. Don't be afraid to show your emotions; but above all, don't ever lie to your team and they'll never lie down.

Dan Devine

I admired Dan Devine. I also had great respect for his coaching skills. Dan didn't get the full respect he deserved until after the Faust years. It was sad that it came down that way, but the demise of Gerry Faust was the rise of Dan Devine.

Dave Duerson
strong safety (1979–82)

How that man survived what he went through without drinking is something I'll never understand. Whenever I see Coach Faust, I get a mental picture of him running up and down our sideline before a crucial third-down play, hollering at everybody, "Say a Hail Mary!" He got so emotionally wound up, I sometimes worried about him.

Allen Pinkett
tailback (1982–85)

Maybe Gerry Faust was too nice a guy to chop off some heads when he should have. But a lot of Notre Dame people figured that it was just too big a jump from high school coaching into this kind of hot seat.

Joe Doyle

FAST FACT: *Faust, succeeding Dan Devine beginning in 1981, came directly from (Cincinnati) Moeller High School, where he produced a 174–17–2 record over 21 years.*

The legend of Lou, right next to Knute Rockne's 105 wins, is as secure as the bricks and mortar of Notre Dame Stadium.

Bob Logan
on Lou Holtz, second only to Rockne in Irish annals, with 100 victories

Lou Holtz is a coach's coach.

Joe Paterno
legendary Penn State head coach

Some coaches are born winners, and I've been around long enough to spot one when I see him. Lou Holtz is one of the chosen few.

Edward "Moose" Krause
tackle (1931–33)/athletic director (1950–81)

You have to have a dream. When you stop dreaming and just try to preserve what you have, you become the hunted, no longer the hunter.

Lou Holtz

oach Holtz is tough, but he knows how to get a team ready for every game. He makes us work hard, and we do it, because he works harder. This man gets inside your head and pushes you to do things the way he wants them done.

Chuck Lanza
center (1984–87)

The coach had all kinds of ways to motivate us. What he wanted to do was bring us together. Every player had to find his own way to reach his potential. If he didn't make that effort, somebody willing to pay the price would take his place in the lineup.

Darrell "Flash" Gordon
*defensive end (1985–88),
on Lou Holtz*

We never went into a Saturday thinking that we wouldn't win. But I can honestly tell you there was never a time on a Sunday or Monday when I didn't think we were quite capable of losing the football game that weekend. I don't care who we played. I coached scared to death. People in the media wanna say that's poor-mouthing? I say it's giving praise, respect, and dignity to the opposition. And that's the first thing you better do. You'd better respect your opponent.

Lou Holtz

When you stop trying to get better, the enthusiasm and the energy begin to drain away from whatever the task might be.

Lou Holtz

When you're coaching at Notre Dame,
you're going to be attacked no matter
what you do.

Lou Holtz

One thing about Notre Dame is that history
repeats itself. That's why you saw this
thing with Lou Holtz coming (his resigna-
tion). Because Lou Holtz is Frank Leahy. Lou
Holtz is Knute Rockne. I mean, everything
shows that had Rockne not died in that plane
crash, he probably would have been fired or
eased out. And we all know they basically fired
Leahy. Because the overriding theme at Notre
Dame is this: We do not want the football program to overshadow the university.

Terrence Moore
Atlanta Constitution *columnist*

WE AREN'T WHERE WE SHOULD BE.
WE AREN'T WHERE WE ARE GOING TO BE.
WE AREN'T WHERE WE OUGHT TO BE.
BUT THANK GOD WE AREN'T WHERE WE
USED TO BE.

Favorite Lou Holtz motto

The only poll I read is the last one every season.

Lou Holtz

If somebody had to mold a Rockne and a Leahy, they couldn't have come up with a better man than Lou Holtz. He *is* Notre Dame.

Dick Rosenthal
athletic director (1987–95)

Any Notre Dame football coach finds something new to worry about every day. But the only thing he should worry about is winning. Ara Parseghian told me that when I took this job. He was right.

Bob Davie
head coach (1997–2001)

Coaching is teaching. Humor is just one of many motivational tools. It's easier to get a point across with a light touch now and then.

Ty Willingham

If you're doing the right thing, it doesn't matter how bright the lights are. If you're doing the wrong thing, it only takes a flashlight.

Ty Willingham

Tyrone Willingham was a dispassionate man at a passionate school.

Pat Forde

When it comes to winning the hearts and minds of his players and Notre Dame Nation, Charlie Weis is doing all the right things.

Pat Forde

Charlie Weis is the first Notre Dame coach to win his first two games on the road since Knute Rockne in 1918.

Associated Press

following the Irish's 17–10 victory over Michigan, September 10, 2005. The previous week, the Weis era debuted with a victory at Pittsburgh

---

If I answered by dignifying that, Bill Parcells and Bill Belichick would humiliate me.

Charlie Weis

*head coach (2005-),
on what it felt like to tie the great Rockne's above-mentioned 87-year-old record—
opening a Notre Dame coaching tenure with consecutive road wins*

Charlie Weis has enough Super Bowl jewelry to open his own Zale's. Weld the four of them together (one from the New York Giants, three from the New England Patriots) and you'd have the world's most valuable set of gold knuckles.

Gene Wojciechowski
ESPN.com

On the day before 10-year-old Montana Mazurkiewicz, named for Joe, died of brain cancer, Notre Dame coach Charlie Weis visited him and let him call the first play vs. Washington in 2005. Even from the Irish 1, Weis sent in Montana's pass. Brady Quinn completed it. Yesterday, Montana's family got a game ball. God bless Charlie Weis.

Ivan Maisel
"Ivan Maisel's 3-Point Stance,"
ESPN.com

Charlie Weis

H e said "What are we going to do?" I said "We have no choice. We're throwing it to the right."

Charlie Weis

to quarterback Brady Quinn,

*on the promise Weis had made to dying
10-year-old Montana Mazurkiewicz before the
Washington game to let the youngster call the
first play of the game, a pass right.
As circumstances played out, the Irish took over
the ball at their own 1, thus sparking Quinn's
concern. The Irish quarterback then passed to
tight end Anthony Fasano, good for a 13-yard
pickup. Weis later sent a game ball autographed
by the team to the Mazurkiewicz family.*

FAST FACT: Young Montana died the day before the game and never got to see his successfully called play. Furthering the family's grief eight months later, Montana's mother also died of cancer.

N ever let them think you're happy, because if they think you are happy then they start to loosen up. You just keep your foot on their throat the whole time.

Charlie Weis

his prescription to counter a letdown for an upcoming opponent

C harlie Weis isn't afraid to tap into his inner leprechaun.

Pat Forde

THE GREAT NOTRE DAME QUARTERBACKS

Many schools have had football teams named Desire. In 1956 Notre Dame had a football team named Hornung. He did everything. He ran. He kicked. He passed. He tackled. He intercepted passes. Surrounded by the walking wounded, playing for a team crippled by injuries, Hornung was the whole show.

Dick Schaap

on the 1956 Paul Hornung-led Fighting Irish that went 2–8, the only Heisman winner in history to play for a losing team

Gus Dorais was a wonderful passer, as good as you ever saw.

Jesse Harper
*head coach (1913–17),
on the brilliant early Irish quarterback, renowned
for his extraordinary passing that upset Army in
1913*

Harry Stuhldreher sounded like a leader on the field. Even as a freshman, he was a good, fearless blocker and was mentally sharp. He went on to become a master of sound quarterback play. He could read through another team's strategy without a key to the code.

Knute Rockne
on the quarterback of the Four Horsemen

C omparing Harry Stuhldreher with Frank Carideo, Rockne once cracked, is like trying to "compare Caesar with Napoleon."

Ray Robinson

I can't recall a Notre Dame quarterback who wasn't a good faker—and Frank Carideo was the best.

Grantland Rice

H e could run, pass, and kick. He was my coach on the field in 1929 and 1930.

Knute Rockne
*on two-time consensus All-America
quarterback Frank Carideo*

W hen Frank Carideo came to Notre Dame, Rockne acknowledged that he knew little about angle punting and thus refused to tamper with Carideo's style. "Do it your way," he told the young man. Carideo would develop into one of the most skilled corner kickers of his day.

Ray Robinson

No one even knew my name, but I was going to practice every day. Running on the seventh team you get disillusioned. Then overnight Leahy seemed to say, "We've got to go with someone who throws the ball," and thank God he did.

Angelo Bertelli
*on starting at tailback as a sophomore
in 1941*

I wasn't much of a runner. I would be at the tailback position, and when I wasn't faking or handing off, I would go back and throw a pass. Otherwise, a tailback in the single wing is a guy that always runs— I never ran.

Angelo Bertelli

In all of Notre Dame's history there was no finer passer than Angelo Bertelli.

Jack Connor

W e were listening in a hut at Parris Island. There were five of six Notre Damers sitting around this Philco radio. We thought Notre Dame won. Then Great Lakes scores and we're crying. We're actually crying. Then a guy walks up to me as I leave the hut. He hands me a telegram. It says I just won the Heisman Trophy. I didn't know whether to laugh or keep on crying.

Angelo Bertelli
*on the final game of the 1943 season,
in which undefeated Notre Dame fell to Great
Lakes Naval Station, 19–14. Despite the tough
loss—the Irish led until a 46-yard touchdown pass
in the final 28 seconds—Notre Dame was voted
the top team in
the country*

FAST FACT: *Bertelli only played in the first six games of his senior season—his Heisman season—before being called into the Marines.*

Angelo Bertelli couldn't run over a speed bump. But with his powerful arm and clever faking, he led the Irish in passing in 1941.

Steve Delsohn

Bertelli was a great quarterback. He had a touch like a feather. He was a very good ball handler and a great faker. He was the best I ever played with. John Lujack was also great and a better all-around player.

Bob Kelly
halfback (1943–44)

He was as sharp a passer as Notre Dame ever had. He could throw the ball with great accuracy. He had so much control over the ball, more than I ever thought of having.

Johnny Lujack
on Angelo Bertelli

I loved playing both ways. I never wanted to come out of the game. If I could play 60 minutes, that was fine. I just wanted to be in there—I loved it. Somebody asked me, "Did you enjoy playing offense more than defense?" I don't know. I just liked them both and wanted to do both. I know that I never wanted to come out of a football game.

Johnny Lujack

Johnny Lujack won four letters his sophomore year (1943), only the third Notre Dame man ever to accomplish the feat, and the first to do it in over 30 years. George Ratterman, another quarterback and a teammate of Lujack's in 1946, would also win letters in four different sports a few years later.

Jack Connor

UNIVERSITY OF NOTRE DAME

Johnny Lujack

In his three years of varsity football, Johnny Lujack starred on three national championship teams (1943, 1946, and 1947). He led the team in passing all three years; he was called the best defensive player in football; he was a consensus All-American two years; he came in third in the Heisman balloting as a junior, and was the winner as a senior. He was elected to the College Football Hall of Fame in 1960.

Jack Connor

Johnny Lujack distinguished himself quickly, running and tackling so hard Leahy knew his name the first week of practice.

Steve Delsohn

People talk about Joe Montana. He had those championship rings from the NFL. He and Bill Walsh had a lot of success together in San Francisco. But Montana, very frankly, couldn't carry Johnny Lujack's shoes.

Bill Fischer

He's probably the greatest all-around athlete I've ever seen in college football. . . . He was just a very tough guy from western Pennsylvania. It probably showed the most when Lujack played defense. He'd come up and hit people head-on. You take Bertelli, myself, or Ratterman? We'd get killed if we went to hit somebody.

Frank Tripucka
quarterback (1945–48),
on Johnny Lujack

P eople were tired of war, so they couldn't get enough of sports. And since Notre Dame was winning all those games, we were a big attraction. And Lujack was our biggest star. This was also before television. So Lujack became a star on the radio. You could hear him make a great run, but you couldn't see him. So you had to use your own imagination. That meant there was some mystery to him. And that made Johnny Lujack even more famous.

Jack Connor

H e's the greatest all-around football player it has been my pleasure to coach.

Frank Leahy
on Johnny Lujack

I never gave winning the Heisman a single thought. All our guys felt that way. All the honors that came to people like George Connor and Bill Fischer? Nobody followed that stuff. Nobody talked about it after practice. Hell, I didn't know until I graduated what my stats were. I didn't know my punting average. I didn't know if I threw for 50 percent. But I knew we won 'em all at Notre Dame.

Johnny Lujack

Ralph Guglielmi is a quarterback who has been extravagantly labeled "a better passer than Angelo Bertelli, a better field general than Johnny Lujack, and more daring than Bob Williams."

Joe Doyle
Sport *magazine,*
October 1954

H e just couldn't have any friends who ever played end. The way he makes the end commit himself, it's just impossible for the defense to cover. Even when he's on the way down, a flip lateral gets him more yardage.

Oklahoma alumnus
on 1954 consensus All-America quarterback Ralph Guglielmi, after Notre Dame downed the Sooners, 28–21, in the 1953 season opener

I wanted to find out for myself if I could play with the best. Everybody knows Notre Dame signifies the best. I wanted to follow in the footsteps of Frank Carideo, Angelo Bertelli, Johnny Lujack, Frank Tripucka, Bob Williams, and Ralph Guglielmi.

Paul Hornung
quarterback (1954–56)

T he women were after him like mice on cheese. He was a good-looking guy. He had this full crop of hair. They called him the Golden Boy.

Dick Prendergast
*end (1955–57),
on Paul Hornung*

P aul probably had more girlfriends than any guy in Notre Dame history. I mean, there weren't any girls *at* Notre Dame. But there were St. Mary's girls. There were South Bend girls. In Paul's case, there were probably Chicago girls and Los Angeles girls too.

Jim Morse
halfback (1954–56)

Paul can do anything. He was *the* outstanding prospect I've seen at Notre Dame—in football, basketball, and baseball. If he'd concentrated on his studies, he'd have graduated *cum laude*. If he'd concentrated on golf, he'd be another Arnold Palmer. If he'd concentrated on the violin, he'd be another Heifetz. He's a natural.

Moose Krause

Paul Hornung won Notre Dame's fifth Heisman trophy. But Hornung didn't deserve it. Not with three touchdown passes and 13 interceptions. And not on a 2–8 team.

Steve Delsohn

University of Notre Dame

Paul Hornung

P aul Hornung will be the greatest quarter-back Notre Dame ever had. He runs like a mower going through grass. Tackles just fall off him. His kicking—why when he reported to me as a freshman, he could punt 80 yards and place-kick over the crossbar from 70 yards.

Frank Leahy

I n his final college game, Paul Hornung had to play halfback because of two dislocated thumbs; he couldn't properly handle the snap from center. But he still gained 215 all-purpose yards, including a 95-yard kickoff return for a touchdown.

Steve Delsohn

Quarterback John Huarte, who had been used by [former head coaches] Hugh Devore and Joe Kuharich as a holder for extra points and field goals, won the 1964 Heisman Trophy a full month before he received his first varsity letter.

Mike Celizic

He went from being a non-monogram winner to being a Heisman winner. John Huarte was a senior when I got there. But he had barely played. I told John before our opener at Wisconsin, "You're my quarterback. I don't care if you throw five interceptions in the first quarter. You're our best quarterback. You're better than any quarterback I've ever had."

Ara Parseghian
*on the Irish QB who starred spectacularly
in his senior season of 1964*

H e's the finest quarterback I've ever been associated with. For speed of the ball, distance, trajectory, and relative accuracy, he's got the finest arm I've ever seen in college football.

Tom Pagna
on Terry Hanratty

J oe Theismann was a freshman when I was a sophomore. He was running the prep squad one day at spring practice. Well, I just buried him. I hit him as hard as I've probably hit anyone. And what did this kid weigh? About 155, 160? Well, not only did Theismann get up, he started mouthing off. I thought: *Hmmm. Very interesting.*

Mike McCoy
defensive tackle (1967–69)

T he most striking thing to me was Joe Theismann's ability to come up with the clutch plays under the most adverse conditions. I remember so vividly a game we had against Southern Cal in 1970 during an absolute deluge. You couldn't believe how terrible the field was.

Ara Parseghian

FAST FACT: In that game at the L.A. Coliseum, Theismann set the all-time Notre Dame single-game mark of 526 passing yards, completing 33 of 58 passes.

T hey both seemed to have a sixth sense. They feel pressure without seeing it.

Tom Pagna

*on legendary Irish QBs Joe Theismann
and Joe Montana*

Joe Theismann was more of a riverboat gambler. He led the parade. He was like the Pied Piper who always said, "Follow me." Joe Montana was more like Cool Hand Luke. He's the guy you would picture at high noon with his hand on the trigger. When he walked on the field, you had the feeling that everything was all right.

Roger Valdiserri
former Notre Dame
sports information director

If you walked into a crowded room, Theismann would be the first person you'd see. You'd have to find Montana.

Roger Valdiserri

There were six registered miracles in Joe Montana's time at Notre Dame, enough to elevate anyone to the rank of blessed.

TIME magazine

Joe Montana

I 'm certain I was pretty rough on him, probably too rough, but I wanted him to realize that he had to improve and give himself the best chance he could to become the best football player he could be. He had entered spring drills as the last quarterback on the depth chart, and yet he was the starter in the spring game. I knew I had uncovered a gem and just had to find a way to polish it.

Dan Devine
on second-year QB Joe Montana

What I was most impressed with regarding Joe was that he was one of those special young men who almost always found a way to win.

Dan Devine
on Montana

I have to give Joe Montana an A+ for leadership. His maturation was obvious.

Dan Devine

⤥

If I were the owner or CEO of a pro football team or had an expansion club, and the ruling was that I could have for my first pick a choice of all the current players in the NFL and all of the players coming out of college, I would use that number-one pick for Joe Montana.

Dan Devine

FAST FACT: NFL player personnel directors ignored Devine's opinion. San Francisco wound up taking the cool Irish quarterback, but not until the third round of the NFL draft.

MAJOR
MOMENTS

T here occurred the damndest crash of bodies I ever heard. When the ref dug everybody out, Ernie Nevers's head was over the line but the ball was under his chest—four inches from the goal!

Harry Stuhldreher
quarterback (1922–24)/
member of the Four Horsemen backfield,
on the key defensive stop of Notre Dame's
27–10 Rose Bowl victory over Stanford in 1925

W hile the Army game was not all-important to Army, it was the supreme test of our playing careers.

Knute Rockne

on the 35–13 upset of the powerful Cadets in 1913. Notre Dame, relatively unknown nationally until that game, shocked the nation and the sport as a whole with the legendary Gus Dorais-to-Rockne passing clinic

W ith Army charging to stop the run, Gus Dorais began flinging graceful spirals to his ends and backs. After missing his first two throws, he hit either 13 or 14 (accounts vary) of his next 15 passes for 243 yards. Any quarterback in any day would gladly have those numbers, but in 1913 it was if aliens had landed in Times Square.

Mike Celizic

I raced across the Army goal line as Dorais whipped the ball and the grandstands roared at the completion of the 40-yard pass. Everybody seemed astonished. There had been no hurdling, no plunging, no crushing of fiber and sinew, just a long-distance touchdown by rapid transit. At the moment that I touched the ball, life for me was complete.

Knute Rockne

FAST FACT: The 40-yard Dorais-to-Rockne touchdown pass was the longest pass completion in college football history at that time.

The whole town turned out. Brass bands, red fire engines, speeches, as if we had repulsed and conquered an attack upon the West by the East.

Knute Rockne
*following the team's return to South Bend after
upsetting Army with the forward pass
in 1913*

In the 1925 Rose Bowl, three of the Four Horsemen played well but the fourth, Elmer Layden, was spectacular, making key runs, belting long punts, and at a crucial moment late in the contest, intercepting a pass and running it back for a TD for the Notre Dame clincher.

Murray Sperber
on the 27–10 victory over Stanford and Ernie Nevers that gave Notre Dame its first-ever national championship

It was the greatest goal line stand any team of mine ever made because the toughest line-smasher in the world was coming at us.

Knute Rockne
on the gritty Irish fourth-quarter stop of Stanford's Ernie Nevers in the 1925 Rose Bowl

ERNIE NEVERS VS.
THE FOUR HORSEMEN

"What a game he played! He could do everything. He tore our line to shreds, ran the ends, forward passed, and kicked."

Knute Rockne wasn't gushing praise about one of his celebrated Four Horsemen, but rather an opposing player: Stanford's immortal fullback Ernie Nevers, who guided Pop Warner's successful double-wing attack in an unforgettable Rose Bowl meeting with the Fighting Irish on New Year's Day 1925.

Entering the game on what amounted to two broken ankles, a heavily taped up Nevers courageously rushed for 114 yards, more than Notre Dame's vaunted Four Horsemen combined. However the Fighting Foursome ultimately prevailed, with fullback Elmer Layden scoring three of the Irish's four touchdowns, two of them on interception returns of Nevers's passes.

With Stanford trailing 20–10 in the fourth quarter, the play of the game occurred—a stoic fourth-down stop of the relentless Nevers from the half-foot line by the great Notre Dame defensive front. The Irish went on to win their first-ever bowl appearance, 27–10.

I t was fantastic. It was unbelievable. It was high drama, worthy of the best talents of a Broadway playwright or a Hollywood scriptwriter!

Irven Scheibeck
writer, Columbus Dispatch,
on the historic come-from-behind 18–13 win over Ohio State in 1935. The Buckeyes carried a 13–0 lead into the fourth quarter, but Notre Dame, behind the passing and running of halfback Andy Pilney, scored three touchdowns, two in the final two minutes, to edge OSU. The winning TD, a 19-yard pass from halfback Bill Shakespeare to end Wayne Millner, came with 40 seconds to go

oth Notre Dame and Army had scoring opportunities inside the 16-yard line. Both could have won the game—and probably the national championship—by kicking a field goal. But neither team even tried one. This included the series in the second quarter when the Irish had a first down at the Army 12. Then, on fourth-and-one at the 3, Billy Gompers came up short on a running play.

Steve Delsohn
*on the 1946 Army–Notre Dame 0–0 tie
at Yankee Stadium*

rank Leahy didn't believe in kicking field goals. If you couldn't ram it in, he thought taking three points would be an insult. He thought Notre Dame was too tough for that.

Jim Mello
on the 0–0 Army-Notre Dame classic of '46

Doc Blanchard slashed through and was loose! He lumbered like a high-speed tank and in a brilliant burst past the secondary he had pierced the entire defense —except for the safetyman, Johnny Lujack. Doc swerved toward the south sideline and gauged the yardage between him and the point of contact with the tackler. At the final instant, he dragged and then drove but Johnny wouldn't be fooled. The Notre Dame safety came in with a head-on collision, but as he wrapped his arms he slid down. Doc started to pull away when Johnny grabbed one foot and tripped him up.

Jim Beach
Daniel Moore
authors,
on the big play of the 0–0 thriller with Army in
'46, one of the all-time classics in college football
history

UNIVERSITY OF NOTRE DAME

Johnny Lujack tackles Army's Doc Blanchard in the 1946 scoreless tie.

It was 1952 or 1953. I would always go into the coaches' room before practice while they were getting ready to go outside. One day Leahy was sitting there, lost in thought. Then he said out loud, "If only we'd kicked the field goal." Six or seven years later, and he's thinking about the goddamn scoreless tie.

Joe Doyle

Those who saw this game witnessed what could be a once-in-sports-history event. They saw four Heisman winners on the same field. Doc Blanchard of Army won it in 1945 and his teammate, Glenn Davis, was the winner in 1946. From Notre Dame, John Lujack won the Heisman in 1947 and Leon Hart in 1949.

Jack Connor
on the legendary 0–0 tie with Army in 1946

T he game-tying pass looks good, but out of nowhere comes Notre Dame linebacker Jerry Groom, who hurls himself into the air and intercepts the ball. Kyle Rote is finally stopped; the goal defended.

Mike Shields

on the furious comeback by SMU that nearly upset Notre Dame, December 3, 1949. Down 20–7 in the last quarter, Rote passed and ran his Mustangs to a tying touchdown, before the Irish scored a final time. The relentless Rote yet again drove his team down to the Notre Dame 4 before finally misfiring, and the Irish's 38-game unbeaten streak and quest for a third national championship title in four years remained intact with the 27–20 victory

Johnny Lattner

J ohn Lattner was the key to our game. He intercepted a pass that looked like a sure touchdown and then ran it back 27 yards that set up our second touchdown, which tied the score at 14–14. Late in the game when we were ahead, Lattner recovered an Oklahoma fumble that prevented a touchdown, and we were able to squeeze out a 27–21 victory.

Frank Leahy

on the 1952 win over the Sooners, the first-ever meeting between the two powerhouses. OU was No. 1 in the country at the time

I n the final quarter, Johnny Lattner, having one of the greatest days any Irish player ever had, rammed through for his fourth score. It was one of the worst beatings USC had ever received; a 48–14 drubbing.

Gene Schoor

on the 1953 trouncing of Southern Cal

R ussia's two sputniks collided in mid-air. The sun set in the east. Hitler was discovered alive in Washington, D.C. And Oklahoma University lost a football game.

The Daily Oklahoman

following the immortal 7–0 upset of Oklahoma, November 16, 1957, ending the Sooners' historic 47-game winning streak.
On fourth down from the Oklahoma 3, right half-back Dick Lynch scored the game's only touch-down behind fullback Nick Pietrosante's superb block that cut off two OU defenders

We upset Oklahoma, 7–0. We won that game on spirit. We were extremely pissed off.

Dick Prendergast

on the general disrespect shown toward the Fighting Irish prior to their 1957 clash against the Sooners in Norman, Oklahoma.
Notre Dame pulled off one of college football's major all-time upsets, halting Oklahoma's record 47-game winning streak

Oklahoma hadn't lost in 47 games. Their fans didn't leave for 20 minutes. They didn't even stand up. They just sat there, stunned. Man, that was fantastic.

Ed Sullivan

tackle (1955–57),
on the huge 7–0 upset of the Sooners in 1957

Tony was crying his eyes out after that game. Everybody was. Because everyone knew exactly what it was. We were Cinderella minus one.

Ken Maglicic
on safety Tony Carey, beaten by USC's Rod Sherman for the winning touchdown in the 1964 regular-season finale—the shocking 20–17 loss to the Trojans in the final minute and a half that spoiled ND's national championship bid in Ara Parseghian's first year in South Bend

It was a shocking thing. You felt punched in the stomach.

Ara Parseghian
on the wilting final-game 20–17 loss to USC in 1964

I t was supposed to happen, but when it did, there was a sense of awe.

Don Gmitter
*end (1964–66),
on the performance of emerging sophomore stars
Jim Seymour and Terry Hanratty after the 1966
season-opening victory over Purdue*

T his will be the greatest game since Hector fought Achilles.

Beano Cook
*former ABC Sports publicity chief,
on the 1966 Notre Dame-Michigan State clash
for the national championship*

W e knew it would be a war. It was like when you were a kid and you got challenged by another kid who was just about your size. You knew you had to fight him, but you weren't real happy about it. That was Notre Dame and Michigan State in 1966. It was bone on bone.

Jim Lynch

T he atmosphere was like that of a Super Bowl game today. . . . It was the most highly charged pregame atmosphere I'd ever experienced.

Jerry Markbreit
back judge for the 1966 Spartans-Irish clash and future NFL referee

I t was one of the greatest comebacks in Notre Dame history.

Ara Parseghian
on the 10–10 tie with Michigan State in 1966.
Down 10–0 with three regular starters out with injuries, the Irish fought back against the toughest defense in America
to gain the infamous tie en route to the national championship

T o this day Michigan State says that Coley O'Brien hurt them because he was quicker of foot than Terry Hanratty.

Mike Celizic

on Notre Dame's unplanned quarterback switch during the first quarter of the 1966 ND-MSU classic after Hanratty injured his shoulder

A s it is at the end of all wars, there was really no winner. This was war today, with the colossi of collegiate football, Notre Dame and Michigan State, marshalling their forces, then kicking the bejabers out of one another, only to have victory escape both.

William Gildea

*author/*Washington Post *sportswriter, on the '66 classic*

I n 1946, Frank Leahy and Red Blaik could play to a tie and not have it haunt them forever. In 1966, Ara Parseghian couldn't.

Mike Celizic

O ver the years I've come to see it was a great testimony to both clubs. We played our hearts out. It was a classic game, a real classic. Knute Rockne would have been proud.

Clinton Jones
Michigan State 1966 consensus
All-America halfback,
on the '66 title tilt between Jones's Spartans and
the Fighting Irish

I was psyched up when I went on the field and I'm still psyched up. I'll probably be psyched till the day I die.

Eric Penick
halfback (1972–74),
after scoring the winning touchdown
against USC in 1973 on an 85-yard run for a 23–
14 ND victory

T he scenario was perfect. Alabama was No. 1 and we were No. 3. So the winner would be the national champion. You also had the North against the South, the Catholics against the Baptists, Ara Parseghian against Bear Bryant. Plus you had these two rich football traditions, and this was the first time they had ever played.

Frank Pomarico
guard (1971–73),
on the 1973 Sugar Bowl pairing of Alabama and
Notre Dame. The Irish won a thriller, 24–23

W e beat a great football team, and they lost to a great football team.

Ara Parseghian
following Notre Dame's one-point win over Ala-
bama in the 1973 Sugar Bowl

T om Clements was cool as a cucumber. It's the most important pass of his career, and Clements hits his secondary receiver.

Luther Bradley
strong safety/cornerback (1973, 1975–77),
on the QB's big-play 35-yard pass from his own
end zone to Robin Weber for the critical first
down that enabled the Irish to salt away the 1973
Sugar Bowl over top-ranked Alabama and earn
Notre Dame's ninth national championship

I would be dropping back into our end zone. I could slip and fall on the wet grass. Or Alabama could sack me. Either way, they get a safety and we lose. I said, "Ara, are you sure you want a pass?" Ara said, "Yeah, I'm sure."

Tom Clements
on the play that brought Notre Dame
the 1973 national championship

oming out on the field in the bright sunlight was the most thrilling feeling I have ever experienced. The crowd erupted and showed the world what green means to the Irish.

Dan Devine

on the October 22, 1977, home game against USC, in which Notre Dame, having warmed up in its navy blue jerseys prior to the game, emerged in green jerseys with gold numerals just before kickoff. The Irish buried Southern Cal 49–19 behind Joe Montana's running (two TDs) and passing (two TDs)

e played nearly a perfect game. We stopped Earl Campbell and rolled to a 38–10 win.

Dan Devine

following the 1978 Cotton Bowl victory over the previously undefeated and top-ranked Longhorns

N ever get into a card game with a guy named Ace. Don't spit into the wind. And beware of Notre Dame with a National Championship at stake. Texas learned that lesson again Monday.

Jack Gallagher
Houston Post *writer,*
following Notre Dame's 38–10 destruction
of the top-ranked Longhorns in the 1978
Cotton Bowl. The Irish shut down Heisman Tro-
phy winner Earl Campbell and converted six
turnovers into all 38 points for their 10th national
title

T his beats the Army game of '32. It surpasses the win of '35 at Ohio State. It beats everything.

Moose Krause
on the frozen-turfed 1979 Cotton Bowl game, the
fabled Joe Montana-led comeback that netted the
Irish a spectacular 35–34 win over Houston

M ore than a quarter-century later, New Year's Day, 1979, stands out as the greatest comeback in Notre Dame history.

Bob Logan
John Heisler

on the momentous Joe Montana-led
Cotton Bowl comeback. Down to Houston, 34–
12, with just seven and a half minutes to play,
Montana returned to the game, having been side-
lined by body temperature loss,
to guide Notre Dame to a stirring 35–34 come-
back win, climaxed by a touchdown on the final
play of the game—an 8-yard pass
to receiver Kris Haines. The deciding tension-rid-
den extra point had to be booted twice by kicker
Joe Unis, when the Irish were flagged on the first
conversion try

To be down 37–20 and to win 38–37 as time expires? I don't want to call it astronomical . . . but it was pretty huge.

Tim Brown

wide receiver/punt-kickoff returner (1984–87)/
Heisman Trophy winner (1987),
on the memorable Irish comeback with 12:26 to go
in the 1986 victory over Southern Cal, sparked by
Brown's 56-yard punt return with 2:15 remaining.
The return put Notre Dame in
position for John Carney's decisive field goal and a
one-point win in L.A.

When John Carney kicked it down the middle, it was like Notre Dame was reborn. The fans felt it. Lou realized it.

Ned Bolcar

linebacker (1986–89),
on the impact of Notre Dame's miraculous 38–37
come-from-behind win over USC
in 1986

UNIVERSITY OF NOTRE DAME

Tim Brown

171

CATHOLICS VS. CONVICTS
T-shirt slogan
heralding the 1988 Notre Dame-Miami clash

Notre Dame's dramatic 31–30 victory over top-ranked Miami figures to go down as a game for the ages. On a legendary grass field that has seen its share of great moments in collegiate football lore, this one might have been the best.

Lou Holtz
on the big game of the 1988 national championship season

It was like we could feel all those Irish legends out there. I kept hearing those lines from our fight song about shaking down the thunder and waking up the echoes.

Chris Zorich
during the 31–30 win over Miami in '88

afety Pat Terrell leaped to frustrate [Miami quarterback] Steve Walsh's pass in the left corner of the south end zone at Notre Dame Stadium. Terrell's heroics prevented Miami from stunning the Irish in the final second of a magnificent college football game. The entire 1988 season, as well as a slice of Fighting Irish football history, hung and swung in the balance at that instant.

Bob Logan
John Heisler

on the final play of the '88 Notre Dame-Miami game—Miami's failed two-point conversion try. The Irish upset the No. 1-ranked Hurricanes, propelling ND toward its 11th national championship

Notre Dame led 16–0 before outclassed West Virginia could make a first down. Scoring on four of their first five possessions in Sun Devil Stadium, the Irish turned the Fiesta Bowl into a 34–21 punch-out party.

Bobby Logan
John Heisler
on the 1989 Fiesta Bowl rout of the Mountaineers, assuring Notre Dame of its 11th national championship

I was kind of surprised when they kicked the ball to me the second time.

Raghib "Rocket" Ismail
wide receiver/kick returner (1988–90), on his twin TD kickoff returns against Michigan in 1989, which whisked the Irish to a 24–19 win at the "Big House" in Ann Arbor

I don't think Bobby Bowden failed his team as much as Lou Holtz delivered for his. Holtz was brilliant that day. Notre Dame's attack was diversified, they were incredibly ready, and they were way better than we all realized.

Tim Layden

Sports Illustrated *writer,*
on the epic 31–24 victory over No. 1-ranked
Florida State in South Bend in 1993, giving the
Irish the top spot in the country with only Boston
College remaining in the way of an undefeated
regular season. In the game, the Irish forced Heis-
man Trophy-winning
Seminoles quarterback Charlie Ward to throw his
first interception in 159 passing attempts

F eels like somebody tore my heart out and shot my dog.

Clay Shiver
former Florida State center,
after the No. 1-ranked Seminoles' 31–24 loss to
Notre Dame, November 13, 1993

Y ou remember in college basketball, when Villanova played out of its head and upset Georgetown? That's how Boston College played against us. Glenn Foley couldn't miss. He could have thrown a BB through a straw. And what did their tight end Pete Mitchell have? Thirteen catches? Ten of them for first downs?

Kevin McDougal
quarterback (1990–93),
on the events of November 20, 1993,
the shocking season-ending 41–39 loss
to Boston College at home that ended
Notre Dame's national championship hopes

I t was a triple play unlike anything a running back had been able to pull off in Notre Dame's storied history.

Bob Logan
John Heisler

on Julius Jones's 200-yard rushing trifecta against Pitt (262 yards, a Notre Dame single-game rushing record), Navy (221 yards), and Stanford (218), during the 2003 season

I s there a wing in the nearby College Football Hall of Fame for the game tape of this one?

Gene Wojciechowski

senior columnist, ESPN.com, on USC's thrilling 34–31 win over Notre Dame in 2005. Southern Cal QB Matt Leinart, "assisted" (translation: pushed from behind) by running back Reggie Bush, ran the ball in from the 1 with seven seconds remaining and no time-outs left to edge the Irish

Y ou're on the 1-yard line. It's man-on-man. It's get in the end zone, or go home.

Matt Leinart
*USC quarterback
and 2004 Heisman Trophy winner,
on the final play of the 2005 Southern Cal-Notre
Dame tilt. Leinart's 1-yard run gave the No. 1-
ranked Trojans a come-from-behind 34–31 victory
that extended USC's winning streak to 28 games*

I t was maddening. I didn't get depressed or anything like that, but it was maddening.

Kayle Buchanan
*BYU cornerback,
following QB Brady Quinn's 2005 aerial assault
on the Cougars that netted a 49–23 Irish victory.
Quinn threw a Notre Dame record six touchdown
passes, four of them to wide receiver Maurice Sto-
vall, which set yet another Irish mark*

THE NOTRE DAME ALL-TIME TEAM

*P*aul Hornung, Tim Brown, Angelo Bertelli, John Huarte, Ralph Guglielmi, Dave Casper, Bob Dove, Nick Eddy, Joe Montana, the Four Horsemen—and those are just some of the legends who didn't *make it!* The irony of every all-time team is that those not selected are often more conspicuous than those icons chosen. But imagine asking four Heisman Trophy winners to take a place on the pine! That's some serious depth.

Inevitably, the task of picking an all-time unit becomes an exercise in creativity. For instance, one of the greatest quarterbacks in Fighting Irish history makes our team as a specialist, where amazingly, after 76 years, he still holds three Notre Dame all-time punt return marks.

Through the ages, Irish fans have witnessed a wealth of superb teams and other-worldly athletes. Perhaps no greater gathering of college football talent has ever been assembled.

THE NOTRE DAME ALL-TIME TEAM

OFFENSE

Tom Gatewood, *wide receiver*
Leon Hart, *tight end*
Aaron Taylor, *tackle*
Bill Fischer, *guard*
Adam Walsh, *center*
Tom Regner, *guard*
George Kunz, *tackle*
Jim Seymour, *wide receiver*
Johnny Lujack, *quarterback*
George Gipp, *running back*
Johnny Lattner, *running back*
Craig Hentrich, *punter*

DEFENSE

Ross Browner, *defensive end*
George Connor, *defensive tackle*
Chris Zorich, *defensive tackle*
Alan Page, *defensive end*
Jim Lynch, *linebacker*
Bob Crable, *linebacker*
Jerry Groom, *linebacker*
Todd Lyght, *cornerback*
Luther Bradley, *strong safety*
Jeff Burris, *free safety*
Clarence Ellis, *cornerback*
John Carney, *kicker*
Frank Carideo, *punt returner*
Raghib "Rocket" Ismail, *kick returner*

Knute Rockne, *coach*

TOM GATEWOOD
Wide receiver (1969–71)
Consensus All-American (1970)

Notre Dame's all-time leading receiver, Tom Gatewood, as a junior in 1970, was the second leading receiver in college football with 77 catches for 1,123 yards and seven touchdowns, which set school records for receptions (still standing) and yardage in a single season. In Notre Dame's 24–11 victory over Texas in the Cotton Bowl, Gatewood caught a 26-yard touchdown pass. A team captain in 1971, he had another outstanding year and was named first-team All-America by *Time*. The New York Giants selected Gatewood in the fifth round of the 1972 draft.

Joe Layden

LEON HART
Tight end (1946–49)
Consensus All-American (1948, '49),
Heisman Trophy (1949),
Associated Press Male Athlete of the Year (1949),
Maxwell Award (college player of the year, 1949),
College Football Hall of Fame (1973)

H e was a big freshman, he weighed about 260 pounds. We tried to fool him on a couple of plays and he wasn't very foolable. We knew he was going to be a great player.

Johnny Lujack
on Leon Hart

H ow could you not do well running behind linemen like Leon Hart?

Terry Brennan

I n winning the award, end Leon Hart became the third Notre Dame player to receive the Heisman Trophy and only the second lineman in the history of the award ever to be so honored (Larry Kelley of Yale won it in 1936).

Jack Connor

AARON TAYLOR
Tackle (1990–93)
Consensus All-American
(1992 at guard/1993 at tackle),
Lombardi Award (nation's top lineman, 1993)

When we needed to find running room, the backs learned to follow number 75, clearing a path for us.

Ray Zellars
*fullback (1991–94),
on Taylor*

BILL FISCHER
Guard (1945–48)
Consensus All-American (1947, '48),
Outland Trophy (nation's top interior lineman, 1948),
College Football Hall of Fame (1983)

Bill Fischer ended his four years at Notre Dame by being selected as the recipient of the Outland Trophy. He was the starting left guard on teams that were undefeated and which won two National Championships. For a big man he had speed, agility, and quickness. He put these assets to good use in becoming one of the nation's premier blocking guards, and on defense he was unmovable.

Jack Connor

ADAM WALSH
Center (1922–24)
College Football Hall of Fame (1968)

W alsh was the heart and soul of the Seven Mules, a group of linemen who made it possible for the Four Horsemen to run free. In a heroic effort against Army his senior season, he played nearly the entire game with two broken hands. Despite this handicap, he did not make a single bad snap from center and even intercepted a pass late in the fourth quarter to secure a six-point Notre Dame victory. After the game, Rockne declared Walsh's performance the greatest he had ever seen by a center. Walsh was also a pivotal figure in a memorable goal-line stand that helped the Irish defeat Stanford, 27–10, in the 1925 Rose Bowl.

Joe Layden

TOM REGNER
Guard (1964–66)
Consensus All-American (1966)

T om Regner, who was listed in the program at 240 but bent the scales at 270, was a certified monster blocker.

Mike Celizic

GEORGE KUNZ
Tackle (1966–68)
Consensus All-American (1968)

Initially a tight end, the versatile Kunz, through injuries to the offensive line, was switched to offensive tackle. The move proved fruitful: Kunz was selected co-captain of the 1968 Irish team and became a consensus All-America. He was also a first-team CoSIDA Academic All-American in '68. The second overall pick in the 1969 draft (Atlanta), Kunz established himself as one of the premier offensive linemen of his generation, being named to the Pro Bowl eight times in a nine-year span.

JIM SEYMOUR
Wide receiver (1966–68)
First team UPI All-American (1967, '68)

H e can "juke" his hips, dip his shoulder, toss his head, flutter his eyelashes, and leave a safety man twisted up like a pretzel as he cuts downfield for a pass.

TIME **magazine**
on Seymour,
October 28, 1966

I went back to pass and got hit as I threw. This thing just quacked and quacked its way downfield, but Jim Seymour flew up in the air and caught it anyway. I thought: Holy Cow. This guy can make me look great.

Terry Hanratty
on his first touchdown pass as a collegian, against Purdue in the 1966 season opener. The Hanratty-Seymour passing-receiving tandem became an instant part of Irish folklore with their performance in that game

JOHNNY LUJACK
Quarterback (1943, 1946–47)
Consensus All-American (1946, '47),
Timmie Award (Touchdown Club of
Washington, D.C., college back of the year, 1947),
College Football Hall of Fame (1960)

Johnny Lujack was one of the greatest signal callers in college football history. In addition, he may have been the greatest defensive back ever to play college football. He was an amazing athlete. At 6 feet and 190 pounds, he had everything a coach could want: speed, power, a great throwing arm, toughness, an uncanny ability to be around the ball, great running instincts, durability, and, above all, a fierce competitive spirit. He was the kind of player who could have been an All-American at any position.

Jack Connor

GEORGE GIPP
Running back (1917–20)
First team All-American (1920),
College Football Hall of Fame (1951)

I felt the thrill that comes to every coach when he knows it is his fate and his responsibility to handle unusual greatness—the perfect performer who comes rarely more than once in a generation.

Knute Rockne
on George Gipp

I consider Gipp superior to either Jim Thorpe or Red Grange.

Knute Rockne

He remains the most durable icon in Notre Dame's crowded pantheon of legends. He was the greatest all-around athlete in the school's history.

Ray Robinson
on the great Gipp

JOHNNY LATTNER
Running back (1951–53)

Heisman Trophy (1953),
consensus All-American (1952, '53),
Maxwell Award (1952, '53),
Timmie Award (1953),
College Football Hall of Fame (1979)

Winner of the Maxwell Trophy in 1952, Lattner became the only player in history to take the award twice. John also won the coveted Heisman Award and trophies from the Washington, Detroit, and Cleveland touchdown clubs for being the nations' top collegiate football player.

Gene Schoor

CRAIG HENTRICH
Punter (1989–92)

A rguably the best all-around kicker who ever wore a Fighting Irish uniform, Hentrich set a single-season school record as a freshman by averaging 44.6 yards per punt. The following year he hit all 41 of his extra-point attempts and 16 of 20 field goals for a team-high 89 points (a school record for kickers). He also broke his own school record with an average of 44.9 yards per punt. In his senior year *Football News* named him honorable mention All-America as both a placekicker and punter. He continues a 14-year NFL career with the Tennessee Titans.

Joe Layden

ROSS BROWNER

Defensive end (1973, 1975–77)

Consensus All-American (1976, '77),
Maxwell Award (1977),
Lombardi Award (1977),
Outland Trophy (1976),
College Football Hall of Fame (1999)

One of the most decorated players in Notre Dame history, Browner was a starter at defensive end throughout his freshman season, impressive in light of the fact that the Irish were extremely deep—they went undefeated and captured a national championship. After missing 1974 with an injury, Browner was named Lineman of the Year by United Press International in 1976 and won the Outland Trophy, presented to the top interior lineman in college football. Browner was even better in 1977. A senior tri-captain, he led the Irish to another national championship and won the Maxwell and Lombardi awards. Browner was the eighth player chosen in the 1978 draft (Cincinnati) and played nine years in the NFL.

Joe Layden

GEORGE CONNOR
Defensive tackle (1946–47)
Consensus All-American (1946, '47),
Outland Trophy (1946)

George Connor was given the honor of being selected by the Football Writers Association of America as the first recipient of the Outland Award honoring the outstanding interior lineman in the country.

Jack Connor

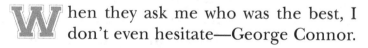

When they ask me who was the best, I don't even hesitate—George Connor.

Jim Martin
end (1946–49)

CHRIS ZORICH
Defensive tackle (1988–90)
Consensus All-American (1989, '90),
Lombardi Award (1990),
Orange Bowl Defensive MVP (1991)

C hris Zorich was so important. He brought in some nastiness that we needed. A lot of teams would not give us respect. They thought Notre Dame was all nice Catholic boys. Zorich showed a lot of people that we would kick some tail.

Pat Terrell

H e was the nicest guy off the field and the biggest maniac on it. Actually, I was kind of scared of Zorich. I just stayed away from him.

Frank Stams
defensive end (1984–88)

O bviously, off the field I'm a different person. On the field, I want to rip someone's head off.

Chris Zorich

ALAN PAGE
Defensive end (1964–66)

Consensus All-American (1966),
College Football Hall of Fame (1993),
Pro Football Hall of Fame (1988)

Page was the sort of physical specimen who made other players think about getting into another sport. . . . He had enormous talent. He could run, he had great quickness, and he had the athletic ability to leap over a blocker and the strength to run through one.

Mike Celizic

JIM LYNCH
Linebacker (1964–66)

Consensus All-American (1966)
Maxwell Award (1966),
College Football Hall of Fame (1992)

Jim Lynch, the team captain and a dogged defender, at 6–1 and 225, was big for a linebacker, bigger than most of the ball carriers he had to tackle. He was an All-American and an academic All-American.

Mike Celizic

Bob Crable
Linebacker (1978–81)
Consensus All-American (1980, '81)

By the time he left South Bend, Crable was widely acknowledged as the finest linebacker ever to wear the uniform of the Fighting Irish. As a sophomore in 1979, he led the team with a school-record 187 tackles (a single-season mark that still stands). As a senior captain in 1981, he capped a remarkable career by making 167 tackles. Crable also holds the Notre Dame record for career tackles (521). A first-round draft pick of the New York Jets in 1982, he suffered several injuries and played only three seasons in the NFL.

Joe Layden

JERRY GROOM
Linebacker (1948–50)
Consensus All-American (1950),
College Football Hall of Fame (1994)

F rank Tripucka gave me the nickname "Boomer" when I was a sophomore. He told the scribes when I hit the ball carrier, the noise went "boom boom" all through the stadium!

Jerry Groom

C aptain of the 1950 Irish squad . . . started at linebacker in both 1949 and '50, helping '49 team to national championship . . . played 465 career minutes—86 percent of the total time Notre Dame played . . . played in 1951 East-West Shrine Game and College All-Star Game . . . first-round selection of Chicago Cardinals in 1951 NFL draft . . . played with Cardinals from 1951–55.

1998 Notre Dame Football Guide

TODD LYGHT
Cornerback (1987–90)
Consensus All-American (1989, '90),
Jim Thorpe Award finalist (1989)

O ne of the most decorated athletes ever to play in the Notre Dame secondary. Lyght became a full-time starter as a sophomore and, as a junior in 1989, became one of the best defensive backs in college football, when he was named a Jim Thorpe Award finalist (best defensive back in America) and unanimous first-team All-America. *The Sporting News* selected him as "the best player in college football" in its 1990 preseason report. Lyght was the fifth player chosen in the 1991 draft and played 12 seasons in the NFL with the Rams (10) and Detroit.

Joe Layden

LUTHER BRADLEY
Strong safety (1973, 1975–77)
Consensus All-American (1977)

B radley was one of Notre Dame's finest defensive players in the 1970s. A member of Notre Dame's 1977 national championship squad, Bradley, a hard-hitting defensive back who had 153 career tackles, also played on Notre Dame's 1973 national championship team as a freshman. He holds the school career record for interceptions, with 17. Against Purdue, in 1975, Bradley returned two interceptions, including a 99-yarder for a touchdown, a play that stands as the second-longest return in Notre Dame history. He was Detroit's first-round draft choice in 1978 and played four years with the Lions.

Joe Layden

JEFF BURRIS
Free safety (1990–93)
Consensus All-American (1993)

One of the more versatile athletes ever to play in the Notre Dame secondary, Burris led the team in interceptions as a junior in 1992, and in 1993, was one of the few players in major college football who made substantial contributions on both sides of the ball. He rushed for six touchdowns from the tailback position, second best on the team. In four years he had 89 tackles and 10 interceptions; he also scored 10 touchdowns. Burris was a first-round draft pick of Buffalo in 1994 and played 10 seasons in the NFL.

Joe Layden

CLARENCE ELLIS
Cornerback (1969–71)

Consensus All-American (1971),
Cotton Bowl Outstanding Defensive Player (1971)

larence Ellis not only played great, but he was black and fast. Normally, USC had all the fast black guys. That's why Clarence made such a dramatic impact. Until he came, Notre Dame's defensive backs were white, slow, and hard-hitting. But you have to catch the guy before you can punish him.

Bob Minnix
halfback (1969–71)

JOHN CARNEY
Kicker (1983–86)

arney, though an all-state kicker, had to make the Fighting Irish as a freshman walk-on in 1983. He holds the Notre Dame record for field goal percentage in a season (.895 in 1984) and a career (.739). His 21 field goals in 1984 is a single-season record and his 51 field goals is a career record. Carney continues his 18-year NFL career.

Joe Layden

FRANK CARIDEO
Punt returner (1928–30)
Consensus All-American (1929, '30),
College Football Hall of Fame (1954)

Frank Carideo, who came to Notre Dame with a reputation as a precision punter, was unanimous All-America in 1929 and '30 and one of the major reasons the teams those years were national champions. He stood 5–7, weighed a little more than 170, and while punting was his specialty, he is on the record books as one of Notre Dame's great punt-kick-off return men.

John D. McCallum

RAGHIB "ROCKET" ISMAIL
Kick returner (1988–90)
Consensus All-American (1990),
Orange Bowl Notre Dame MVP (1990)

That kid is the fastest I've ever seen. He's faster than the speed of sound.

Bo Schembechler
*Michigan head coach (1969–89),
on Rocket Ismail*

KNUTE ROCKNE
Head coach (1918–30)
Consensus national championships (1924, 1929, 1930),
College Football Hall of Fame (1951)

I n the Roaring Twenties, when sports icons were as potent as bathtub gin, Knute Rockne of Notre Dame was to college football what Babe Ruth was to baseball, what Jack Dempsey was to boxing, what Bill Tilden was to tennis, and what Bobby Jones was to golf.

Ray Robinson

T here were the remarkable statistics: Rockne's teams lost only 12 games in 13 years, posted five unbeaten seasons and won three national titles. His lifetime winning percentage of .881 (105–12–5) is still the highest in both college and pro football.

Steve Delsohn

THE GREAT NOTRE DAME TEAMS

I t was almost like we had too many stars. Take a look at the running back position. You had Ricky Watters, Tony Brooks, Reggie Brooks, Jerome Bettis, Rodney Culver, Dorsey Levens. I mean, after that year Dorsey Levens transferred. The guy's an awesome runner. He's balling now for Green Bay. But he couldn't even get on the field for Notre Dame.

Irv Smith
tight end (1989–92),
on the 1990 Fighting Irish

T hat 1924 team—the Four Horsemen and Seven Mules—would always be my favorite team. I think I sensed that that backfield was to be a great one. They were a product of destiny. I suppose they'd been brought together by accident, but it was no accident that made them into one great unit. That was design and hard work.

Knute Rockne

R ock didn't know what it was to lose when he put Frank Carideo in there to run the team in 1929 and 1930. They won 19 straight, were National Champions both seasons, and piled up a total of 410 points to their opponents' 112. Rockne considered that bunch the greatest he ever coached.

Paul Castner

O f all Rockne's teams that passed in review before me, I rate at the top his 1929 and '30 squads. They were undefeated. They played through harder schedules than any previous Notre Dame team. They had tremendous size and mobility. They were nifty when they had to be, and they could turn on power when that was indicated. They had the country at large raving about their individuals as well as their team activity. They ranged through the land defeating everything in sight.

Warren Brown
renowned sports journalist

T he press declared the 1930 edition of Notre Dame football as good, or maybe better, than the Four Horsemen/ Seven Mules team of 1924.

Bill Cromartie
Jody H. Brown

The 1941 season, my sophomore year, we still had the single wing, still the leather helmet, and we were undefeated—the first undefeated Notre Dame team since Rockne's 1930 National Championship season. We were tied by Army in the rain in New York. We ended up third in the nation.

Angelo Bertelli

I think that the 1943 team offensively was maybe the best of the three teams I played on (1943, 1946, 1947). The 1946 team defensively was just tremendous. Our opponents only scored four touchdowns and never made an extra-point try, but I think the '43 team was as good an offensive team as I have ever been on.

Johnny Lujack

They're the greatest Notre Dame football team I've ever seen.

Fritz Crisler
*former Michigan coach and athletic director,
on the 1943 Fighting Irish*

They turned what could have been a disastrous season into one of the most brilliant in Notre Dame's history.

Anonymous sportswriter
*on the 1944 Irish, led by interim coach
Ed McKeever, who fashioned an 8–2 record with
many of Notre Dame's best athletes serving in
the military*

That's one of the greatest, if not the greatest team I've ever seen.

Jeff Cravath
*former USC head coach,
on Notre Dame's 1947 national champions, after
his Trojans fell to the Irish, 38–7*

N otre Dame fielded the greatest college football team in history, but which unbeaten Irish juggernaut was it: the '46 or the '47 squad?

Sports Illustrated

N otre Dame was college football's strongest team—in 1946 and maybe ever.

Steve Delsohn

N otre Dame could lose it first string, its second string, and perhaps even part of its third string—and still remain undefeated.

Anonymous sportswriter
on the 1947 Fighting Irish

I t has guts, it has character. It's the greatest team I've ever coached.

Frank Leahy
on his 1949 Irish squad

In 1949, behind Jim Martin, Leon Hart, and star quarterback, Bob Williams, Notre Dame breezed to a 10–0 record and Leahy's fourth national title. This also concluded the program's most glorious era. Between 1946 and 1949, the Irish played 38 consecutive games without a defeat. They won three of four national championships. The one season (1948) they didn't win it all, they finished No. 2.

Steve Delsohn

They're the strongest Notre Dame team ever.

Chuck Erickson
former North Carolina athletic director,
on the 1966 Fighting Irish

At least 12 of those guys will be drafted by the pros.

Ralph Hawkins
former Army secondary coach,
on the 1966 national champions

T his is the best team by far that I've ever coached. Not only that, it is the best balanced college football team I've ever seen in my life.

Ara Parseghian
on the '66 Irish

A s time goes by, the 1977 national championship that our team won becomes even more meaningful. Though I coached many great teams, only four were able to put themselves in a position to win the national championship, and only my 1977 team actually won it.

Dan Devine

O ur football team is prettier than I am, but that's about it. They don't play pretty at times, but they sure play together as a team.

Lou Holtz
on his 1988 national champions

THE GREAT RIVALRIES

There have been so many great games, but maybe none more memorable than in 1974, when Notre Dame was ahead 24–0 and Anthony Davis ran the second-half kickoff back to ignite an incredible comeback and a 55–24 USC victory.

Lou Holtz
John Heisler

N otre Dame didn't take up football until 1887. . . . The first game was against the University of Michigan (an 8–0 loss). . . . The goodwill between Notre Dame and Michigan lasted exactly one year. In 1888, Michigan arrived for two games played on successive days in the spring. Michigan won the first game handily but narrowly escaped with a win the next day when a Wolverine player picked up the ball during what Notre Dame thought was a timeout and ran with it for the winning goal. The referee, from Michigan, sided with the Wolverines, and the ensuing quarrel was so fierce it took 11 years until the two sides had cooled off sufficiently to play again.

Mike Celizic

W e couldn't fit Notre Dame in. And I might say we don't have a particularly large number of alumni in South Bend, Indiana.

Fritz Crisler

on the discontinuation of the Michigan-Notre Dame series following the 1943 season. The long-held belief is that Crisler so detested Irish coach Frank Leahy that he would not schedule Notre Dame again. The breech existed through Crisler's term as AD at Michigan (1968), after which the two schools reopened negotiations. However, it was not until 1978 that the series finally resumed, a hiatus of 35 years

I t was the type of game that you win 20 times and lose 21 times.

Bo Schembechler
*on Michigan's 29–27 loss to Notre Dame
in 1980*

I t was clear to players and coaches on both sides that the loser of this game was going to be emotionally destroyed. . . . Suffice to say, this was the sweetest of games to win, the bitterest of games to lose.

John Kryk
*author/sportswriter,
on the physical 1980 Notre-Dame-Michigan battle that see-sawed back and forth before Irish
kicker Harry Oliver's desperation 51-yard field goal
ended it*

Pandemonium ensued. Within seconds, Harry Oliver was lost under a green mountain of jubilant teammates and fans alike. Notre Dame Stadium erupted like it had never erupted before. Everyone present knew they had just witnessed once-in-a-lifetime drama. Indeed, it was one of the grandest moments in Notre Dame's storied football history. A miracle field goal to cap a miraculous comeback. To beat Michigan. At fabled Notre Dame Stadium. With Touchdown Jesus signaling the kick good on the library mural that overlooks the north end zone. With the Fighting Irish band belting out "The Victory March." It was the quintessence of Notre Dame football.

John Kryk
on the stirring 29–27 victory over Michigan
in 1980

I n what will forever remain one of the most outstanding individual performances in series history, Raghib "Rocket" Ismail blasted off into stardom by returning two kickoffs for touchdowns in the second half, and Notre Dame hung on for a 24–19 victory on a dark, rainy afternoon.

John Kryk
on the 1989 Michigan-Notre Dame game

O kay. I guess they didn't learn anything.

Raghib "Rocket" Ismail
to himself as Michigan elected to kick to him in the fourth quarter of their 1989 meeting, after Ismail had already returned the second-half kickoff 88 yards for a touchdown. The Rocket then zoomed 92 yards with the second kickoff for a remarkable pair of TDs

I grew up a fan of Michigan, and it was sweet to get my first victory against them.

Rick Mirer

*quarterback (1989–92),
on his first career start, September 15, 1990, vs.
the Wolverines at Notre Dame Stadium. Mirer
put the Irish up, 14–3, in the first
quarter, scoring a touchdown, before taking them
76 yards at game's end with an 18-yard TD pass
to Adrian Jarrell to give ND a 28–24 come-from-
behind win*

W ithout exception, all the last-minute thrillers have been played at Notre Dame Stadium, while all the authoritative drubbings have occurred at Michigan Stadium. And neither school has been intimidated when playing on the road.

John Kryk

*on the Michigan-Notre Dame series,
standing at 18–14–1 in favor of the
Wolverines through 2005*

Michigan is our No. 1 game. I think the best way to explain it is that Michigan is a national school, like Notre Dame. It's got alumni all over. Consequently, there's no question in my mind right now that Michigan is *the* game.

Moose Krause
in 1990

Michigan has a lot of tradition and so do we. Every year we put that pride and tradition on our shoulders, and every year we have to go out and prove it.

Chris Zorich

There was always some horrible loss to avenge, even if it happened 20 years ago. For Purdue there was the revenge factor for 1950, when Purdue beat the Irish and broke Frank Leahy's undefeated string at 39 games, and for 1954 when Len Dawson led the Boilermakers to a 27–14 victory and broke Notre Dame's 13-game undefeated streak. But mostly it was revenge for 1965.

Mike Celizic

FAST FACT: The Boilermakers had beaten Notre Dame 25–21 in '65, behind the passing, running, and kicking of triple-threat quarterback Bob Griese, who mentioned to Sports Illustrated: "We could do anything we wanted to against them. It was mechanical."

For 34 years the Army game was the highwater mark on the Notre Dame schedule, and to play in the contest for only one minute was the ambition of every candidate for our team.

Frank Leahy

Perhaps it was an Irish lullaby that lulled Southern California into slumber land where they suffered a hideous nightmare. Maybe it was just an old-fashioned behind-the-barn whipping that scorched the land of Troy and sent its inhabitants reeling into humiliation.

Bill Cromartie
Jody H. Brown
on the 51–0 blowout of USC in 1966

I couldn't imagine or dream of a score like that.

Ara Parseghian
on the 51–0 annihilation of Southern Cal
in the national championship season of 1966, the
widest margin of victory ever over USC
in series history

I hated the USC guys. They lived in California. They never shoveled snow.

Chris Zorich

H ate is too strong a word. But I never liked USC. I didn't like L.A. I didn't like their campus. I didn't like the arrogance of their players. I couldn't stand the galloping Trojan horse, especially when they brought him to South Bend. I mean, this thing defecated all over our field. Then they didn't clean it up. Even the USC band was irritating.

Mike McCoy

A rrogant sons of bitches. That's the way I looked at USC's players. Their fans were not much different. They were arrogant SOBs with swimming pools.

Art Best
halfback (1972–74)

I've learned to appreciate the rivalry with USC and how it fits into the Notre Dame tradition. It means a lot to me. I took it for granted, but now I sometimes pinch myself and realize I was lucky enough to be part of something like that. Coach Faust kept telling us we were fortunate to be there. He was right.

Tim Brown

The loss was tough to take, because it means the seniors will never be able to say "I beat Notre Dame." It's something we'll have to live with the rest of our lives.

Rodney Peete
USC quarterback,
on the 27–10 loss to the top-ranked Irish in 1988,
in which costly turnovers and penalties did in the
No. 2-ranked Trojans

WINNING AND LOSING

I n the first 55 years of the twentieth century, Notre Dame football teams went undefeated in 18 seasons. In 17 others it lost one game. The 15 campaigns in which two defeats had come were regarded as "off" years. The year 1934, with three losses, was "poor." The three years which had seen *four* defeats ('04, '28, '50) were ghastly. The 1933 campaign, the lone losing season (3–5–1), was *atrocious*.

Francis Wallace

I'm aware everybody expects Notre Dame to win every game. For our fans, the only thing more important than winning is breathing.

Lou Holtz

It's unfortunate that when you are winning there is always someone ready to point an accusing finger at you.

Ara Parseghian

Tying is bad, but there's something worse. That's losing.

Ara Parseghian

Perhaps no one took losses harder than I did, and no one got over them sooner than I did. That helped contribute to my winning seasons, realizing that if I lingered too long over one loss, it would affect our preparations for the next week, and then I would be moping about two losses.

Dan Devine

A small percentage of rabid fans always react as though losing a football game is a capital offense.

Gerry Faust

〰

Each of my 26 defeats was a gut-wrenching jolt. None hurt worse than that four-point loss at USC in 1982, because Notre Dame should have been credited with a gallant goal-line stand to preserve a 13–10 victory. Instead, the officials counted the decisive TD when they saw Trojan tailback Michael Harper dive into the end zone. What they didn't see was that Harper was missing some essential baggage in his takeoff across the goal line—the football.

Gerry Faust

FAST FACT: *Harper's fumbled ball turned out to be in the hands of Irish defensive end Kevin Griffith on the 2-yard line, well before the USC ball carrier went airborne for the end zone.*

Winning happens in a lot of other ways. When you're trying to teach young men and turn them into better men, what they become 10 years down the road is much more important.

Gerry Faust

The most difficult loss I've ever been associated with.

Lou Holtz
on blowing a 31–7 lead against Tennessee in 1991, before losing, 35–34. No Notre Dame team had ever blown a 24-point lead in Notre Dame Stadium

I never saw anybody take losses any harder than Lou Holtz. . . . Lou never tried to build up his team too much after a win. He knew what a fine line there is between that and defeat.

George Kelly
linebackers coach (1969–85)/administrator

With just over a minute to go, Eagles quarterback Glenn Foley put together one more miracle drive, setting up possibly the saddest moment in a half-century plus of ups and downs in Notre Dame Stadium.

Bob Logan
John Heisler

on the numbing 41–39 loss to Boston College the week following the big victory over Charlie Ward and Florida State in 1993. The Irish, trailing in the fourth quarter 38–17, fashioned an astonishing comeback to take the lead at 39–38, before the Eagles' David Gordon knuckleballed a left-footed 41-yard field goal to kill Notre Dame's national championship dreams

Losses affected me greatly, but I tried not to take them in the house when I got home.

Dan Devine

H e was so unbelievably intense, he would seem to be in a form of shock. Even from time to time, Frank Leahy would vomit.

Dr. Nicholas Johns
longtime Notre Dame team physician,
on the Irish coaching icon's strong reaction
to losing

I t bothered me when they cut the scholarships. It was like being put on probation by the NCAA. Except your own school was doing it.

Terry Brennan
on the election by ND administrators
Frs. Joyce and Hesburgh to limit football scholar-
ships to just 18 a year, beginning in the early
1950s—a decision that reaped what it sowed by
the 1956 season, when the Irish posted a 2–8
record

Y ou become a victim of your own success. We were 10–2 in 1974. Well, 10–2 under normal circumstances isn't bad. But when you measure it against the undefeated season in 1973, the national championship, you begin to feel like maybe you failed. And losing never gets any easier for you. The hurt and the agony are going to come.

Ara Parseghian

A ra taught me a lesson. It's not about wins and losses. It's not about houses or cars. It's about dignity. It's about how you live your life.

Ken Maglicic

R ockne used to tell us, "One loss is good for the soul, too many losses are not good for the coach."

Paul Castner

T his was a win by the Notre Dame spirit. It was a win by a group of guys who just refused to fold and believed. You can't pick out a hero today. Notre Dame was the hero.

Lou Holtz

on the 31–30 win over No. 1 Miami in 1988 that put the Irish on course for the national championship

I 've never had a victory in my coaching career with a group of guys so dedicated. I'll remember this forever.

Ara Parseghian

following his last game as Notre Dame head coach, January 1, 1975—a 13–11 upset of Alabama in the Orange Bowl that snuffed the Tide's national title hopes for the second consecutive year

When you come back like that, you've got a lot of emotion and you feel pretty good. And then when you can't come through with the victory, there's the ability to have a big letdown.

Brady Quinn

on the 44–41 overtime home loss to Michigan State in 2005. The Irish overcame a 21-point deficit to send the game into OT. In the defeat, Quinn passed for a school-record five touchdowns and career-high 487 yards, the second-highest total in Notre Dame history

To pilfer a phrase from the eminent phrase-maker, Walter Wellesley "Red" Smith, the 1956 Fighting Irish "overwhelmed two opponents, underwhelmed eight, and whelmed none.

Dick Schaap

There are two ways you can go after a loss: You can sit there and feel sorry for yourselves, or you can take that bitter taste in your mouth and say "I don't want to have that taste a year from now."

Charlie Weis

If you're waiting for me to say it was a good loss, you won't hear that here. Losing is losing. There are no moral victories. What I did tell them was not to hang their heads. That was a slugfest, a street fight. That was a good football game.

Charlie Weis
in the aftermath of Notre Dame's last-second 34–31 loss to top-ranked USC in 2005

THE LOCKER ROOM

J ohn wanted to grow bigger and stronger like his idol, Superman. So he went on a cod-liver oil binge and once drank seventeen pints of the stuff in a single week.

Johnny Lattner's mother

Our only concern was playing that football game, winning the national championship, and then having a good spring; trying to get laid and having a couple of beers.

Rocky Bleier
halfback (1965–67)

Terry Hanratty scraped together money by running a barbershop in his dorm room, charging $1 a head and providing an old *Playboy* magazine for the guy waiting his turn in the chair.

Mike Celizic

I couldn't understand why two snot-nosed kids should be on the cover of *TIME*.

Terry Hanratty
on his and Jim Seymour's appearance on the October 28, 1966, cover of the famous weekly, just six weeks into their sophomore seasons at Notre Dame

Nobody throws the ball deep anymore. And if I were playing today, I'd never use a huddle.

Terry Hanratty
in 2004, at age 56

If you come to our stadium, and you look closely at Michigan's 45-yard line, you'll find a jock strap there. That's mine.

Don Lund
*former Michigan halfback,
on Creighton Miller's brilliant move in the
Wolverine secondary that faked Lund out of his
proverbial supporter, en route to a
66-yard touchdown dash in ND's 35–12
victory over Michigan in 1943. Miller rushed for
159 yards on only 10 carries*

There are only two events that could out-draw Notre Dame on New Year's Day—the Second Coming and a Muhammad Ali fight.

CBS television executive
1969

NEW COACH. NEW POPE. NEW ERA.
SAME JESUS.
T-shirt
seen at Notre Dame Stadium in 2005

Notre Dame had a collection of offensive linemen who would go on to play more than a half century of professional ball. Every interior lineman on the team had a pro career. And not one of them could hold a block on George Webster.

Mike Celizic
on the 1966 Irish, who met Michigan State's formidable Webster during the classic 10–10 tie that same year

In all, 25 of the 44 starters for the Spartans and Irish received All-American mention.

Mike Celizic
on the No. 1 Notre Dame and No. 2-ranked Michigan State squads of 1966

O ver the years, since he retired from coach-ing because he was afraid the job would kill him, the question that comes up most is, "Why did you go for the tie?" It's become an obsession for him, his Moby Dick that he keeps sticking harpoons into but can't kill.

Mike Celizic

on Ara Parseghian's eternal torment, the second-guessing critics who continuously bring up the former head coach's final set of decisions at the close of the 1966 Michigan State-Notre Dame game that ended in the infamous 10–10 tie

N otre Dame has never won a national championship without having an All-American defensive end.

Lou Holtz
John Heisler

My biggest message is that the only constant in life is change and you have to be able to adapt to that change and believe in yourself. I tell people you can be the very best you can be; your destiny lies in your own hands.

Rocky Bleier

Before every game, Brady Quinn gulps down a spoonful of honey. It provides a quick burst of energy, although the youngster agrees that victory provides a taste that's even sweeter. The honey is just a habit that goes back to his grade-school days.

**Bob Logan
John Heisler**

You'll burn in hell for this!

Frank Leahy
to center Jim Schrader (1951–53), who once botched a key extra-point snap

In 1989, Notre Dame went 12–1 and Miami went 11–1. But they gave Miami the national championship because it beat Notre Dame that season. When the same thing happened in 1993—and we beat Florida State—they gave it to Florida State.

Jeremy Nau
defensive end/outside linebacker (1991–94)

You don't have to be from Ireland to be Irish.

**1919 edition of *Scholastic*,
Notre Dame campus newspaper**
*defending the reasons behind calling
Notre Dame the "Fighting Irish"*

FAST FACT: *Legendary* Chicago Tribune *sports editor Arch Ward used the term "Fighting Irish" in his pieces for the* South Bend Tribune *in 1920 as a young writer. Later ND student press agent Francis Wallace popularized the nickname in his dispatches.*

For more than 20 years, Moose Krause cared for his wife, Elise, who had suffered brain damage and paralysis in an automobile accident. For the last eight years before she died in 1990, Moose would visit her twice daily in a nursing home to spoon-feed her. In the last months before she died, Moose would go to the nursing home a third time every day to sing her to sleep.

Jack Connor

Pinned down, Rock said he picked the backfield of Frank Carideo, Marchy Schwartz, Joe Savoldi, and Marty Brill as the all-time champs at Notre Dame because they "packed more sheer power than the Four Horsemen team."

Paul Castner

I f you study films of the old Green Bay Pack-ers you'll notice that Vince Lombardi's defensive line play resembled Rock's to a great extent. This was no mere coincidence. Lombardi had been one of Fordham's Seven Blocks of Granite and had been taught by Jimmy Crowley and Frank Leahy—both Rockne students. Lombardi carried on in the great tradition of Rockne, with a minimum of guessing and excessive use of jumping in and out of the line, red-dogging, and what have you.

Frank Carideo

In all the years I played, coached, and have watched football, [halfback] Marty Brill and [quarterback] Frank Carideo were probably the best blockers I've seen.

Marchy Schwartz
halfback (1929–31)/
two-time consensus All-American (1930–31)

I 'm happy for the team, but I worry about their heads.

Charlie Weis

after Notre Dame's second straight victory to open the 2005 season. Weis was clairvoyant. The over-confident Irish lost in overtime at home to Michigan State the following week

S tamp one for the Gipper!

Associated Press

on fans' attempts in October 2005 to get the U.S. Postal Service to issue a stamp honoring George Gipp

N otre Dame is bigger than any of us.

Frank Leahy

NOTRE DAME NATIONAL CHAMPION ROSTERS

*W*hile most followers of the Fighting Irish feel it's been way too many moons since the last national championship season, no college in the country can boast more titles than the men of the Golden Dome. These are the names from all the glory years—Notre Dame's eleven consensus national championship teams. Like all heroes who have fought the good fight, they've earned their special place, never to be forgotten: The champion Blue and Gold.

1924
10—0—0
(includes 27–10 Rose Bowl victory over Stanford)
Knute Rockne, *head coach*

	Pos	Wt	Exp	High School
Arndt, Russell	C	170	2 yrs	Mishawka (Ind.) High
Bach, Joseph	**T**	**188**	**1 yr**	**Chisholm (Minn.) High**
Boland, Joseph	T	220	1st yr	Catholic High (Phila., Pa.)
Cerney, William	FB	164	2	Ignatius (Chicago, Ill.)
Collins, Charles	E	167	2	Ignatius Academy
Coughlin, Bernard	HB	144	1	Wasecs (Minn.) High
Crowe, Clement	**E**	**180**	**1**	**Lafayette (Ind.) High**
Connell, Ward	B	169	2	Notre Dame Prep
Crowley, James	**LHB**	**157**	**2**	**Green Bay (Wis.) High**
Eaton, Wilbur	E	155	2	Creighton High (Omaha, Neb.)
Edwards, John	B	152	1st yr	Kiski
Glueckert, Charles	G	177	2	South Bend High
Hanousek, Richard	G	177	1st yr	St. Thomas School
Harrington, Vincent	G	165	2	Sioux City High
Harmon, Joseph	C	160	2	Catholic High (Ind.)
Hearndon, John	B	160	2	Green Bay (Wis.) High
Huntsinger, Edward	**E**	**170**	**2**	**Chillocothee High**
Kizer, Noble	**G**	**160**	**2**	**Plymouth (Ind.) High**
Layden, Elmer	**FB**	**161**	**2**	**Davenport (Iowa) High**
Livergood, Bernard	B	171	2	Stonington (Ill.) High
Miller, Don	**RHB**	**158**	**2**	**Defiance (Ohio) High**
Miller, Edgar	**T**	**178**	**2**	**Canton (Ohio) High**
Miller, Gerald	B	137	2	Defiance (Ohio) High
O'Boyle, Harry	B	176	1st yr	East Des Moines (Iowa) High
Reese, Frank	B	150	2	Robinson (Ill.) High
Scherer, Edward	B	146	1st yr	Scott High (Toledo, Ohio)
Stuhldreher, Harry	**QB**	**148**	**2**	**Kiski**
Walsh, Adam (Capt.)	**C**	**187**	**2**	**Hollywood High**
Weibel, John	**G**	**165**	**2**	**Erie High**

Starters in bold

1929
9–0–0
Knute Rockne, *head coach*

Name	Pos	Name	Pos
Bailie, Roy	E	**Leahy, Frank**	**T**
Bloemer, Bernard	G	Listzwan, Tom	FB
Bondi, Gus	G	Locke, Joseph	G
Brannon, Bob	LHB	Lyons, James	G
Brill, Marty	**RHB**	Mahaffey, Thomas	G
Cannon, Dan	RHB	Mahoney, Henry	E
Cannon, John	**G**	Manley, John	T
Carberry, John	E	Massey, Robert	G
Carideo, Frank	**QB**	McManmon, Art	T
Carmody, James	T	McNamara, Regis	T
Cassidy, William	G	Metzger, Bert	G
Cavanaugh, Vince	C	**Moynihan, Tim**	**C**
Christman, Norb	QB	**Mullins, Lawrence**	**FB**
Collins, Ed	E	Murphy, Emmett	QB
Colrick, John	**E**	Murphy, Tom	E
Conley, Tom	E	Nash, Joseph	C
Conway, Pat	FB	O'Brien, Ed	LHB
Cronin, Carl	RHB	O'Brien, John	E
Culver, Al	T	O'Connor, Paul	FB
Donoghue, Bernard	LHB	Piggott, Robert	FB
Donoghue, Richard	T	Provissiero, Phil	G
Elder, John	**LHB**	Reiman, Fred	C
Gebert, Al	QB	Rogers, John	C
Griffin, James	E	Savoldi, Joe	FB
Grisanti, Al	E	Schwartz, Charles	T
Herwit, Norman	G	Schwartz, Marchmont	LHB
Host, Paul	E	Seymour, Albert	G
Howard, Al	FB	Shay, George	FB
Izo, George	T	Thornton, Joe	T
Kaplan, Clarence	RHB	**Twomey, Ted**	**T**
Kassis, Tom	G	**Vezie, Manfred**	**E**
Keeney, Bernard	QB	Vlk, George	E
Kenneally, Tom	QB	Wharton, T.	T
Kersjes, Frank	E	Whelan, Vince	G
Koken, Michael	LHB	Williams, Aubrey	FB
Kosky, Frank	E	Yarr, Thomas	C
Kremer, Theodore	FB	Yelland, John	C
Law, John	**G**	Zoss, Abe	G
Leahy, Bernard	LHB		

1930
10–0–0
Knute Rockne, head coach

	Pos		Pos
Bailie, Roy	E	Kosky, Frank	E
Brill, Marty	**RHB**	**Kurth, Joe**	**T**
Butler, Frank	C	Leahy, Bernard	LHB
Carideo, Frank	**QB**	Lukats, Nick	HB
Conley, Tom (Capt.)	E/FB	Mahoney, Henry	E
Cronin, Carl	QB/HB	McManmon, Art	T
Culver, Al	**T**	McNamara, Regis	T
Donoghue, Richard	T	**Metzger, Bert**	**G**
Greeney, Norm	G	**Mullins, Lawrence**	**FB**
Hanley, Dan	HB/FB	Murphy, Emmett	QB
Harris, Jim	G	O'Brien, John	E
Hoffmann, Frank	T	O'Connor, Paul	FB
Host, Paul	E	Pierce, Bill	G
Howard, Al	FB	Rogers, John	C
Jaskwhich, Chuck	QB	**Schwartz, Marchmont**	**LHB**
Kaplan, Clarence	RHB	Sheeketski, Joe	RHB
Kassis, Tom	**G**	Terlaak, Bob	G
Kersjes, Frank	G	Vlk, George	E
Koken, Michael	LHB	**Yarr, Thomas**	**C**

1943
9–1–0
Frank Leahy, head coach

	Pos		Pos
Adams, John W.	RT	Mieszkowski, Edward T.	LT
Angsman, Elmer J.	LH	**Miller, Creighton**	**LH**
Berezney, Peter Jr.	LT	Palladino, Robert F.	RH
Bertelli, Angelo B.	**QB**	**Perko, John F.**	**RG**
Cibula, George	LT	Rellas, Chris S.	RE
Coleman, Herbert E.	**C**	Renaud, Charles	LG
Curley, Robert M.	LT	Ruggiero, Frank A.	LT
Czarobski, Zygmont	**RT**	**Rykovich, Julius A.**	**RH**
Dancewicz, Frank J.	QB	Signaigo, Joseph S.	RG
Davis, Raymond	LH	Skat, Alvin C.	QB
Earley, Frederick J.	RH	Snyder, James	FB
Filley, Patrick J. (Capt.)	**LG**	Statuto, Arthur J.	C
Flanagan, James	LE	Sullivan, George A.	LT
Ganey, Michael	RT	Szymanski, Francis S.	C
Hanlon, Robert S.	FB	Terlep, George	QB
Kelly, Robert J.	RH	Tharp, James L.	LT
Kuffel, Raymond	LE	Todorovich, Marko S.	RE
Krupa, Edward Harry	RH	Trumper, Edward	RE
Kulbitski, Victor J.	FB	Urban, Gasper G.	LG
Limont, Paul J.	**LE**	Waldron, Ronayne	QB
Lujack, John	QB	**White, James J.**	**LT**
Lyden, Michael P., Jr.	C	**Yonakor, John J.**	**RE**
Mello, James A.	**FB**	Zilly, John L.	RE
Meter, Bernard	RG		

1946
8–0–1
Frank Leahy, head coach

	Pos	Ht	Wt	Exp	Hometown
Agnone, John	LH	5–8	170	2	Youngstown, Ohio
Ashbaugh, Russell	QB	5–9	175	2	Youngstown, Ohio
Begley, Gerald	QB	6–1	165	1st yr	Yonkers, N.Y.
Brennan, James	RH	5–8	165	1	Milwaukee, Wis.
Brennan, Terence	**LH**	**6–0**	**175**	**1**	**Milwaukee, Wis.**
Brown Roger	QB	5–11	185	1st yr	Chicago, Ill.
Brutz, Martin	RG	5–11	208	1	Niles, Ohio
Budynkiewicz, Ted	T	6–0	220	1st yr	Chicopee, Mass.
Cifelli, August "Gus"	LT	6–4	225	1st yr	Philadelphia, Pa.
Clatt, Corwin	FB	6–0	200	1	E. Peoria, Ill.
Connor, Charles	LG	5–10	200	1st yr	Chicago, Ill.
Connor, George	**LT**	**6–3**	**225**	**1st yr**	**Chicago, Ill.**
Coutre, Lawrence	LH	5–8	175	1st yr	Chicago, Ill.
Cowhig, Gerald	LH	6–3	211	1	Dorchester, Mass.
Creevy, John	FB	6–2	215	1	Clawson, Mich.
Czarobski, Zygmont	**RT**	**6–0**	**213**	**2**	**Chicago, Ill.**
Dougherty, James	C	6–2	180	1st yr	Woodlyn, Pa.
Earley, Fred	RH	5–7	165	2	Parkersburg, W. Va.
Espenan, Ray	LE	6–2	195	1st yr	New Orleans, La.
Fallon, John	RT	6–0	210	2	Alton, Ill.
Fischer, William	**LG**	**6–2**	**225**	**1**	**Chicago, Ill.**
Flanagan, James	RE	6–1	187	1	West Roxbury, Mass.
Frampton, John	LG	5–11	190	1st yr	Pomona, Calif.
Gompers, William	RH	6–1	180	1	Wheeling, W. Va.
Hart, Leon	RE	6–4	225	1st yr	Turtle Creek, Pa.
Heywood, William	QB	6–0	190	1st yr	Providence, R.I.
Higgins, Luke	RG	6–0	208	1	Edgewater, N.J.
Kosikowski, Frank	RE	6–0	205	1st yr	Milwaukee, Wis.
LeCluyse, Leonard	FB	5–11	188	1st yr	Kansas City, Mo.
Limont, Paul	LE	6–2	200	2	Pittsfield, Mass.
Livingstone, Robert	LH	6–0	175	1	Hammond, Ind.
Lujack, John	**QB**	**6–0**	**180**	**1**	**Connellsville, Pa.**
Martin, James	**LE**	**6–2**	**205**	**1st yr**	**Cleveland, Ohio**
Mastrangelo, John	**RG**	**6–1**	**210**	**2**	**Vandergrift, Pa.**

	Pos	Ht	Wt	Exp	Hometown
McBride, Robert	RG	6–0	205	2	Lancaster, Ohio
McGee, Coy	HB	5–9	163	1st yr	Longview, Tex.
McGehee, Ralph	RT	6–1	210	1st yr	Chicago, Ill.
McGurk, James	FB	6–1	195	2	Montclair, N.J.
McNichols, Austin	C	6–0	193	1st yr	Chicago, Ill.
Mello, James	**FB**	**5–10**	**185**	**2**	**W. Warwick, R.I.**
Meter, Bernard "Bud"	RG	5–11	190	2	Cleveland, Ohio
Michaels, William	E	6–1	190	1st yr	Girard, Ohio
O'Connor, Wm. "Zeke"	LE	6–4	215	1	Ft. Montgomery, N.Y.
O'Connor, Wm. "Bucky"	LG	6–0	195	1	Tulsa, Okla.
Panelli, John "Pep"	FB	5–11	190	1	Morristown, N.J.
Potter, Thomas	LG	5–10	190	1	Kearney, N.J.
Ratterman, George	QB	6–0	165	2	Cincinnati, Ohio
Rovai, Fred	RG	6–0	200	2	Hammond, Ind.
Russell, Wilmer	LT	6–4	220	1	Omaha, Neb.
Schuster, Kenneth	LT	6–2	215	1	Chicago, Ill.
Scott, Vincent	LG	5–8	210	2	LeRoy, N.Y.
Signaigo, Joseph	LG	6–0	200	1	Memphis, Tenn.
Simmons, Floyd	RH	6–0	195	1	Portland, Ore.
Sitko, Emil "Red"	**RH**	**5–10**	**185**	**1st yr**	**Ft. Wayne, Ind.**
Skoglund, Robert	LE	6–1	198	2	Chicago, Ill.
Slovak, Emil	RH	5–7	155	2	Eliston, Ohio
Smith, Wm. L.	LH	5–11	165	1st yr	Lebanon, Ky.
Statuto, Arthur	C	6–1	215	1	Saugus, Mass.
Strohmeyer, George	**C**	**5–9**	**195**	**1st yr**	**McAllen, Texas**
Sullivan, George	RT	6–3	210	2	E. Walpole, Mass.
Swistowicz, Michael	RH	5–11	190	1st yr	Chicago, Ill.
Tobin, George	G	5–10	195	1	Arlington, Mass.
Tripucka, Frank	QB	6–0	180	1	Bloomfield, N.J.
Urban, Gasper	LT	6–1	215	1	Lynn, Mass.
Vangen, Willard	C	6–1	205	1st yr	Bell, Calif.
Walsh, Robert	LE	6–2	200	1st yr	Chicago, Ill.
Walsh, William	C	6–2	210	1	Phillipsburg, N.J.
Wendell, Martin	C	5–9	200	1	Chicago, Ill.
Wightkin, William	RE	6–2	200	1	Detroit, Mich.
Zalejski, Ernest	LH	5–11	180	1st yr	South Bend, Ind.
Zilly, John	**RE**	**6–2**	**200**	**2**	**Southington, Conn.**
Zmijewski, Al	RT	6–1	215	1st yr	Newark, N.J.

1947
9–0–0
Frank Leahy, head coach

	Pos	Ht	Wt	Exp	Hometown
Ashbaugh, Russell	QB	5–9	175	2	Youngstown, Ohio
Begley, Gerald	QB	6–1	170	1	Yonkers, N.Y.
Brennan, James	RH	5–8	160	2	Milwaukee, Wis.
Brennan, Terence	**LH**	**6–0**	**173**	**2**	**Milwaukee, Wis.**
Brown, Roger	QB	5–11	180	1	Chicago, Ill.
Budynkiewicz, Theodore	RT	6–0	205	1	Chicopee, Mass.
Burnett, Albert	E	6–2	195	1st yr	Irvington, N.J.
Carter, Donald	C	6–3	200	1st yr	Detroit, Mich.
Ciechanowicz, Emil	T	6–4	230	1	Chicago, Ill.
Cifelli, August "Gus"	T	6–4	225	1	Philadelphia, Pa.
Clatt, Corwin	FB	6–0	200	2	E. Peoria, Ill.
Connor, George (Capt.)	**LT**	**6–3**	**220**	**1**	**E. Chicago, Ill.**
Connor, John	G	6–0	185	1	Chicago, Ill.
Couch, Leo	G	5–9	200	1st yr	South Bend, Ind.
Coutre, Lawrence	HB	5–8	170	1	Chicago, Ill.
Czarobski, Ziggy	**RT**	**6–0**	**213**	**3**	**Chicago, Ill.**
Dailer, James	G	5–9	180	1	Wheeling, W. Va.
Earley, Fred	HB	5–8	170	3	Parkersburg, W. Va.
Espenan, Raymond	E	6–2	189	1	New Orleans, La.
Fallon, Joseph	G	5–11	190	1st yr	Alton, Ill.
Fischer, William	**LG**	**6–2**	**230**	**2**	**Chicago, Ill.**
Frampton, John	G	5–11	190	2	Pomona, Calif.
Gaul, Frank	G	5–10	200	2	Cleveland, Ohio
Gay, William	HB	5–10	180	1st yr	Chicago, Ill.
Gompers, William	RH	6–1	175	2	Wheeling, W. Va.
Grothaus, Walter	C	6–2	197	1	Cincinnati, Ohio
Hart, Leon	**RE**	**6–4**	**216**	**1**	**Turtle Creek, Pa.**
Helwig, John	T	6–2	198	1st yr	Los Angeles, Calif.
Helwig, Joseph	G	6–2	200	1st yr	Los Angeles, Calif.
Hudak, Edward	T	6–2	200	1st yr	Bethlehem, Pa.
Johnson, Frank	E	5–11	185	1st yr	Cincinnati, Ohio
Kosikowski, Frank	RE	6–0	202	1	Milwaukee, Wis.

	Pos	Ht	Wt	Exp	Hometown
Lally, Robert	G	6–0	185	1	South Euclid, Ohio
LeCluyse, Leonard	FB	5–11	188	1	Kansas City, Mo.
Leonard, William	E	6–2	190	1	Cleveland, Ohio
Lesko, Alex	E	6–0	180	2	Homestead, Pa.
Livingstone, Robert	LH	6–0	168	2	Hammond, Ind.
Lujack, John	**QB**	**6–0**	**180**	**2**	**Connellsville, Pa.**
Martin, James	**LE**	**6–2**	**205**	**1**	**Cleveland, Ohio**
McCarty, Thomas	FB	6–1	185	1	Trenton, N.J.
McGee, Coy	LH	5–9	165	2	Longview, Texas
McGehee, Ralph	LT	6–1	211	1	Chicago, Ill.
Michaels, William	E	6–1	190	1	Girard, Ohio
O'Connor, Wm. "Bucky"	RG	5–11	196	2	Tulsa, Okla.
O'Connor, Wm. "Zeke"	E	6–4	200	2	Ft. Montgomery, N.Y.
Oracko, Steve	G	6–0	193	1	Lansford, Pa.
Panelli, John "Pep"	**FB**	**5–11**	**190**	**2**	**Morristown, N.J.**
Russell, Wilmer	T	6–4	200	2	Omaha, Neb.
Saggau, Thomas	HB	6–0	170	1	Dennison, Iowa
Schuster, Kenneth	T	6–3	210	2	Chicago, Ill.
Signaigo, Joseph	RG	6–1	205	2	Memphis, Tenn.
Simmons, Floyd	FB	6–0	195	2	Portland, Ore.
Sitko, Emil "Red"	**RH**	**5–8**	**175**	**1**	**Ft. Wayne, Ind.**
Smith, Lancaster	LH	5–10	165	1	Lebanon, Ky.
Spaniel, Frank	HB	5–10	180	1st yr	Vandergrift, Pa.
Statuto, Arthur	C	6–2	200	2	Saugus, Mass.
Strohmeyer, George	C	5–9	195	1	McAllen, Texas
Sullivan, George	RT	6–3	206	3	E. Walpole, Mass.
Swistowicz, Michael	FB/HB	5–11	175	1	Chicago, Ill.
Tripucka, Frank	QB	6–0	178	2	Bloomfield, N.J.
Urban, Gasper	T-G	6–0	200	2	Lynn, Mass.
Walsh, William	**C**	**6–3**	**205**	**2**	**Phillipsburg, N.J.**
Waybright, Douglas	E	6–0	180	1	Saugus, Mass.
Wendell, Martin	**RG**	**5–10**	**198**	**2**	**Chicago, Ill.**
Wightkin, William	RE	6–2	205	1	Santa Monica, Calif.
Wilke, Clifford	HB	6–0	190	1st yr	Hamilton, Ohio
Zmijewski, Alfred	T	6–1	200	1	Newark, N.J.

1949
10—0—0
Frank Leahy, head coach

	Pos	Ht	Wt	Yr	Hometown
Banicki, Frederick	T	5–10	190	So	Chicago, Ill.
Barrett, William C.	HB	5–8	179	So	Chicago, Ill.
Bartlett, James J.	C	6–3	196	So	Cincinnati, Ohio
Begley, Gerald C.	QB	6–1	175	Sr	Yonkers, N.Y.
Boji, Byron B.	C	5–11	186	So	Chicago, Ill.
Burns, Paul E.	**MG**	**6–2**	**205**	**So**	**Athens, Pa.**
Bush, John L.	FB	6–0	185	So	Davenport, Iowa
Caprara, Joseph A.	FB	6–0	198	So	Turtle Creek, Pa.
Carter, Thomas	QB	5–11	173	Jr	Los Angeles, Calif.
Cifelli, August "Gus"	T	6–4	230	Sr	Philadelphia, Pa.
Connor, John F.	E	6–0	190	Sr	Chicago, Ill.
Cotter, Richard A.	HB	6–1	178	Jr	Austin, Minn.
Coutre, Lawrence E.	**HB**	**5–9**	**170**	**Sr**	**Chicago, Ill.**
Dailer, James H.	G	5–9	185	Sr	Wheeling, W. Va.
Daut, John D.	T	6–1	205	So	Hempstead, N.Y.
Dickson, George C.	QB	5–11	170	Sr	S. Pasadena, Calif.
Dolmetsch, Robert E.	E	6–2	195	So	Chicago, Ill.
Espenan, Ray	E	6–2	188	Sr	New Orleans, La.
Feigl, Charles	C	6–1	185	Jr	Chicago, Ill.
Flynn, William	E	6–2	197	Jr	Gary, Ind.
Gander, Fidel J.	FB	6–1	190	So	Chicago, Ill.
Gay, William T.	**DB**	**5–10**	**168**	**Jr**	**Chicago, Ill.**
Groom, Jerome P.	**MLB**	**6–3**	**210**	**Jr**	**Des Moines, Iowa**
Grothaus, Walter J.	**C**	**6–2**	**192**	**Sr**	**Cincinnati, Ohio**
Hamby, James H.	C	6–1	195	So	Caruthersville, Mo.
Hart, Leon (co-Capt.)	**RE**	**6–4**	**245**	**Sr**	**Turtle Creek, Pa.**
Helwig, John F.	**LLB**	**6–2**	**194**	**Jr**	**Los Angeles, Calif.**
Higgins, William P.	G	5–11	180	Jr	Chicago, Ill.
Hovey, William A.	HB	5–10	175	So	Lake Placid, N.Y.
Huber, Thomas E.	T	6–2	195	Jr	Milwaukee, Wis.
Hudak, Edward J.	T	6–2	200	Sr	Bethlehem, Pa.
Huml, Donald	E	6–1	190	So	Chicago, Ill.

	Pos	Ht	Wt	Yr	Hometown
Johnson, Frank A.	**G**	**6–0**	**195**	**Sr**	**Cincinnati, Ohio**
Johnston, Frank A.	G	5–8	184	So	Chicago, Ill.
Jonardi, Raymond C.	E	6–2	188	Jr	Pittsburgh, Pa.
Kapish, Robert J.	E	6–0	187	So	Barberton, Ohio
Kiousis, Martin J.	G	5–11	190	So	Lakewood, Ohio
Koch, David A.	E	6–2	190	So	Wayzata, Minn.
Lally, Robert J.	**G**	**6–0**	**185**	**Sr**	**Cleveland, Ohio**
Landry, John W.	FB	6–1	180	Jr	Rochester, N.Y.
Mahoney, James E.	T	6–1	204	Jr	Erie, Pa.
Martin, James E. (co-Capt.)	**T-E**	**6–2**	**204**	**Sr**	**Cleveland, Ohio**
Mazur, John E.	QB	6–1	185	So	Plymouth, Pa.
McGehee, Ralph W.	**T**	**6–1**	**202**	**Sr**	**Chicago, Ill.**
McKillip, Leo	HB	5–10	175	Jr	McCook, Neb.
Modak, Daniel	G	6–1	197	So	Campbell, Ohio
Mutscheller, James F.	E	6–1	194	So	Beaver Falls, Pa.
Nusskern, Jack	T	6–2	215	Sr	West View, Pa.
O'Hara, John	HB	5–9	180	So	Lewiston, N.Y.
O'Neil, John D.	FB	6–0	185	So	Aurora, Ill.
Oracko, Stephen F.	G	6–0	185	Sr	Lansford, Pa.
Ostrowski, Chester C.	E	6–1	196	So	Chicago, Ill.
Perry, Arthur R	G	5–11	198	So	Davenport, Iowa
Petitbon, John E.	**S**	**5–11**	**180**	**So**	**New Orleans, La.**
Sitko, Emil "Red"	**RH-FB**	**5–8**	**180**	**Sr**	**Ft. Wayne, Ind.**
Smith, Eugene F.	HB	5–9	170	Jr	LaCrosse, Wis.
Spaniel, Francis J.	**HB**	**5–10**	**184**	**Sr**	**Vandergrift, Pa.**
Swistowicz, Michael	**DB**	**5–11**	**195**	**Sr**	**Chicago, Ill.**
Toneff, Robert	**DT**	**6–1**	**232**	**So**	**Barberton, Ohio**
Wallner, Frederick W.	**RLB**	**6–2**	**208**	**Jr**	**Greenfield, Mass.**
Waybright, Douglas G.	E	6–1	186	Sr	Saugus, Mass.
Whiteside, William A.	QB	5–10	172	Jr	Philadelphia, Pa.
Wightkin, William J.	**E**	**6–2**	**204**	**Sr**	**Culver City, Calif.**
Williams, Robert A.	**QB**	**6–1**	**180**	**Jr**	**Baltimore, Md.**
Yanoschik, Phillip	C	6–0	195	Jr	Conemaugh, Pa.
Zalejski, Ernest R.	FB	5–11	185	Jr	South Bend, Ind.
Zambroski, Anthony J.	G	5–11	196	So	Erie, Pa.
Zancha, John D.	T	5–10	195	So	Chicago, Ill.
Zmijewski, Alfred A.	T	6–1	200	Sr	Newark, N.J.

1966
9–0–1
Ara Parseghian, head coach

	Pos	Ht	Wt	Yr	Hometown
Alexander, Harry W.	T	6–1	240	Sr	Wilmington, Del.
Azzaro, Joseph Richard	K	5–11	190	Sr	Pittsburgh, Pa.
Bars, Michael L.	T	6–4	230	So	Farmington, Mich.
Bartholomew, William	LB	6–2	212	So	Glen Mills, Pa.
Belden, Robert F.	QB	6–2	205	So	Canton, Ohio
Bleier, Robert "Rocky"	**HB**	**5–11**	**185**	**Jr**	**Appleton, Wis.**
Burgener, Michael Amos	HB	5–10	182	Jr	Marion, Ill.
Collins, Leo	LB	5–11	200	Sr	Fargo, N.D.
Conjar, Lawrence Wayne	**FB**	**6–0**	**212**	**Sr**	**Harrisburg, Pa.**
Criniti, Frank	HB	5–8	173	So	Charleston, W. Va.
Dainton, William Charles	G	6–2	220	Jr	Gary, Ind.
Dickman, Daniel D.	G	6–0	210	Jr	Pittsburgh, Pa.
Duranko, Peter N.	**DT**	**6–2**	**235**	**Sr**	**Johnstown, Pa.**
Earley, Michael Henry	E	6–0	200	So	South Bend, Ind.
Eddy, Nicholas M.	**HB**	**6–0**	**195**	**Sr**	**Lafayette, Calif.**
Fischer, Ray	G	6–1	220	So	Cleveland, Ohio
Fournier, Louis John	T	6–3	248	Jr	Cheboygan, Mich.
Fox, Roger	G	5–11	230	So	Rockford, Ill.
Franger, Michael Craig	QB–HB	5–11	185	So	Elkhart, Ind.
Freebery, Joseph James	LB	6–0	207	So	Wilmington, Del.
Furlong, Thomas Edward	E	6–2	205	Jr	Cleveland, Ohio
Gladieux, Robert Joseph	HB	5–11	185	So	Louisville, Ohio
Gmitter, Donald A.	**E**	**6–2**	**210**	**Sr**	**Pittsburgh, Pa.**
Goeddeke, George A.	**C**	**6–3**	**228**	**Sr**	**Detroit, Mich.**
Gorman, Timothy John	G	5–11	220	Sr	Hoboken, N.J.
Grable, Charles Anthony	LB	6–0	215	Jr	Oshkosh, Wis.
Hagerty, Robert	FB	6–3	230	Sr	Mingo Junction, Ohio
Haley, David Francis	HB	5–11	190	Jr	Hingham, Mass.
Hanratty, Terrence Hugh	**QB**	**6–1**	**190**	**So**	**Butler, Pa.**
Hardy, Kevin Thomas	**DT**	**6–5**	**270**	**Jr**	**Oakland, Calif.**
Harshman, Daniel Ryan	HB	6–0	190	Jr	Toledo, Ohio
Heaton, Michael Joseph	E	6–2	205	Jr	Seneca, Ill.
Heneghan, Curtis Joseph	E	6–3	190	So	Redmond, Wash.
Holtzapfel, Michael	HB	6–1	200	So	Ironton, Ohio
Horney, John	LB	5–11	205	Sr	Youngstown, Ohio
Jeziorski, Ronald Martin	G	5–10	210	Sr	South Bend, Ind.
Kelly, Gerald Thomas	C	6–1	205	Sr	Los Angeles, Calif.
Kelly, James	HB	6–0	195	Sr	Rutherford, N.J.
Konieczny, Rudolph A.	T	6–0	225	Jr	Fairview, Mass.
Kuechenberg, Robert John	**T**	**6–2**	**225**	**So**	**Hobart, Ind.**
Kunz, George James	E	6–5	228	So	Arcadia, Calif.

	Pos	Ht	Wt	Yr	Hometown
Kuzmicz, Michael Anthony	T	6–4	235	Jr	South Bend, Ind.
Landolfi, Charles C.	HB	5–11	204	So	Elfwood, Pa.
Lauck, Charles Bernard	E	6–1	220	So	Indianapolis, Ind.
Lavin, John Patrick	LB	6–4	200	So	Spokane, Wash.
Leahy, James	C	6–0	220	So	Lake Oswego, Ore.
Lium, John D.	C	6–4	230	Sr	Bronx, N.Y.
Lynch, James (Capt.)	**ILB**	**6–1**	**225**	**Sr**	**Lima, Ohio**
Malone, Michael Patrick	C	6–3	226	So	Elmira, N.Y.
Marsico, Joseph Anthony	G	6–0	220	Sr	River Forest, Ill.
Martin, David Kenneth	**OLB**	**6–0**	**210**	**Jr**	**Roeland Park, Kan.**
May, Paul Albert	FB	5–10	205	Jr	Alexandria, Va.
McGill, Michael Ray	**OLB**	**6–2**	**220**	**Jr**	**Hammond, Ind.**
McKinley, Thomas Michael	G	6–1	218	So	Kalamazoo, Mich.
Meyer, Jack	HB	5–11	170	Sr	Cadillac, Mich.
Monty, Timothy	C	6–0	198	So	St. Albans, W. Va.
Norri, Eric John	T	6–2	240	So	Virginia, Minn.
O'Brien, Coleman C.	QB	5–11	173	So	McClean, Va.
O'Leary, Thomas Michael	**DB**	**5–10**	**185**	**Jr**	**Columbus, Ohio**
Page, Alan	**DE**	**6–5**	**238**	**Sr**	**Canton, Ohio**
Paternostro, Victor John	C	6–1	235	Sr	Lyndhurst, N.J.
Pergine, John Samuel	**ILB**	**6–0**	**210**	**Jr**	**Norristown, Pa.**
Quinn, Stephen T.	C	6–1	215	Jr	Northfield. Ill.
Quinn, Thomas H.	DB	6–1	192	So	Clinton, Iowa
Rassas, Kevin Walter	DB	6–1	190	Jr	Winnetka, Ill.
Regner, Thomas Eugene	**G**	**6–1**	**245**	**Sr**	**Kenosha, Wis.**
Reynolds, Thomas	LB	6–0	185	So	Ogden Dunes, Ind.
Rhoads, Thomas Patrick	**DE**	**6–2**	**220**	**Sr**	**Cincinnati, Ohio**
Ryan, James	K	5–10	185	Sr	Shreveport, La.
Sack, Allen	E	6–3	205	Sr	Boothwyn, Pa.
Schiralli, Angelo Peter	G	6–0	220	Sr	Gary, Ind.
Schnurr, Fred	T	6–3	245	Sr	Cleveland, Ohio
Schoen, Thomas Ralph	**DB**	**5–11**	**178**	**Jr**	**Euclid, Ohio**
Schrage, Patrick Clifford	T	6–0	235	So	Oshkosh, Wis.
Seiler, Paul Herman	**T**	**6–4**	**235**	**Sr**	**Algona, Iowa**
Seymour, James Patrick	**E**	**6–4**	**205**	**So**	**Berkley, Mich.**
Skoglund, William	E	6–1	210	So	LaGrange Park, Ill.
Slettvet, Thomas	FB	6–0	202	So	Sumner, Wash.
Smithberger, James L.	**DB**	**6–1**	**190**	**Jr**	**Welch, W. Va.**
Snow, Paul Francis	E	6–1	180	So	Long Beach, Calif.
Stenger, Brian Francis	E	6–4	210	So	Euclid, Ohio
Swatland, Richard Thomas	**G**	**6–2**	**225**	**Sr**	**Stamford, Conn.**
VanHuffel, Alan	LB	6–2	210	Jr	South Bend, Ind.
Vuillemin, Edward A.	LB-FB	6–1	205	So	Akron, Ohio
Wengierski, Timothy J.	HB	6–0	185	Sr	River Forest, Ill.
Zubek, Robert	E	6–2	220	So	Painesville, Ohio
Zurowski, David Matthew	HB	6–3	190	Sr	Oxon Hill, Md.

1973

11—0—0

(includes 24–23 Sugar Bowl victory over Alabama)
Ara Parseghian, head coach

	Pos	Ht	Wt	Yr	Hometown
Achterhoff, Jay	DT	6–4	245	So	Muskegon, Mich.
Allocco, Frank	QB	6–1	178	Jr	New Providence, N.J.
Alvarado, Joe	C	6–1	239	Sr	East Chicago, Ind.
Andler, Ken	DE	6–6	236	So	Cleveland, Ohio
Arment, Bill	DT	6–4	235	Jr	Muncie, Ind.
Audino, John	FB	5–10	175	Jr	Albany, N.Y.
Bake, Tom	HB	5–10	190	Jr	Middletown, Ohio
Balliet, Calvin	TE	6–4	220	So	Moorestown, N.J.
Barnett, Reggie	**CB**	**5–11**	**188**	**Jr**	**Flint, Mich.**
Bauer, Ed	TE	6–3	238	Jr	Cincinnati, Ohio
Best, Art	**LHB**	**6–1**	**200**	**So**	**Gahanna, Ohio**
Bolger, Tom	G	6–2	239	Sr	Cincinnati, Ohio
Bossu, Steve	C	6–0	210	So	Maple Heights, Ohio
Bradley, Luther	**SS**	**6–2**	**204**	**Fr**	**Muncie, Ind.**
Brantley, Tony	QB	6–0	203	So	Oklahoma City, Okla.
Brenneman, Mark	**C**	**6–4**	**240**	**Sr**	**York, Pa.**
Brown, Cliff	QB	6–0	205	Sr	Middletown, Pa.
Brown, Ivan	LB	6–3	217	So	LeRoy, Ill.
Browner, Ross	**DE**	**6–3**	**247**	**Fr**	**Warren, Ohio**
Bullock, Wayne	**FB**	**6–1**	**233**	**Jr**	**Newport News, Va.**
Casper, Dave	**TE**	**6–3**	**252**	**Sr**	**Chilton, Wis.**
Chauncey, Jim	DB	6–0	174	Jr	Wheat Ridge, Colo.
Clements, Tom	**QB**	**6–0**	**189**	**Jr**	**McKees Rocks, Pa.**
Collins, Greg	**OLB**	**6–3**	**228**	**Jr**	**Troy, Mich.**
Creevey, Tom	LB	6–3	205	Sr	Mishawaka, Ind.
Demmerle, Pete	**SE**	**6–1**	**196**	**Jr**	**New Canaan, Conn.**
Devine, Tom	DE	6–3	240	Sr	Jackson, Mich.
Diminick, Gary	HB	5–9	176	Sr	Mt. Carmel, Pa.
DiNardo, Gerry	**RG**	**6–1**	**242**	**Jr**	**Howard Beach, N.Y.**
Doherty, Brian	P	6–2	192	Sr	Portland, Ore.
Doherty, Kevin	SE	6–0	185	So	Portland, Ore.
Fanning, Mike	**DT**	**6–6**	**270**	**Jr**	**Tulsa, Okla.**
Fedorenko, Nicholas	DT	6–5	260	So	Chicago, Ill.
Fine, Tom	DE	6–5	250	Jr	Apple Valley, Calif.
Galanis, John	DE	6–4	250	So	Ipswich, Mass.
Gambone, John	FB	6–1	207	Sr	Canton, Ohio
Goodman, Ron	HB	5–11	192	Jr	Mount Sinai, N.Y.
Hartman, Pete	C	6–1	244	Sr	San Francisco, Calif.
Hayduk, George	DE	6–3	255	Sr	Factoryville, Pa.
Hein, Jeff	DE	6–1	235	Sr	Cincinnati, Ohio
Hill, Greg	HB	6–0	187	Jr	Pilot Mountain, N.C.
Horton, Kurt	QB	6–2	187	So	New Canaan, Conn.
Kelly, Chuck	FB	5–9	195	Jr	St. Paul, Minn.
Kinealy, Kevin	DB	5–10	166	Sr	St. Louis, Mo.
Kornman, Russ	FB	6–0	205	So	Wauwatosa, Wis.
Lane, Gary	LB	6–0	221	Sr	Kalamazoo, Mich.
Laney, Tom	G	6–2	248	Jr	Sprague, Wash.
Linehan, Paul	HB	6–0	199	So	Dallas, Texas

	Pos	Ht	Wt	Yr	Hometown
Lopienski, Tom	DB	6–1	182	So	Akron, Ohio
Lozzi, Dennis	T	6–3	257	Sr	Whitman, Mass.
Mahalic, Drew	**OLB**	**6–4**	**220**	**Jr**	**Birmingham, Mich.**
Maschmeier, Tom	DB	5–11	185	So	Cincinnati, Ohio
McBride, Mike	T	6–5	246	Sr	Michigan City, Ind.
McDonald, Fran	DB	5–10	163	So	Lindenhurst, N.Y.
McGreevy, Bob	HB	5–9	180	Jr	Delta, Pa.
McGuire, Mike	DB	6–0	189	Jr	Elmhurst, Ill.
Messaros, Robert	G	6–1	228	So	Elyria, Ohio
Miller, Tim	LB	6–2	220	Jr	Pittsburgh, Pa.
Miskowitz, Lew	DT	5–11	230	Sr	Rock Island, Ill.
Morrin, Dan	G	6–3	240	Sr	Croydan, Pa.
Moty, Leonard	DB	6–2	190	So	Shasta, Calif.
Naughton, Mike	DB	6–3	195	Sr	Bloomfield Hills, Mich.
Neece, Steve	**LT**	**6–3**	**245**	**Jr**	**Janesville, Wis.**
Niehaus, Steve	**DT**	**6–5**	**270**	**So**	**Cincinnati, Ohio**
Nosbusch, Kevin	DT	6–4	265	Jr	Milwaukee, Wis.
Novakov, Tony	LB	5–11	205	So	Cincinnati, Ohio
O'Donnell, John	C	6–1	235	Jr	Woodside, N.Y.
Parise, Tom	FB	6–0	208	So	Longmont, Colo.
Parker, Mike	DB	5–11	175	Jr	Cincinnati, Ohio
Payne, Randolph	DB	5–9	185	So	Palmer Park, Md.
Penick, Eric	**RHB**	**6–1**	**195**	**Jr**	**Cleveland, Ohio**
Pohlen, Pat	T	6–4	244	So	Downey, Calif.
Pomarico, Frank	**LG**	**6–1**	**250**	**Sr**	**Howard Beach, N.Y.**
Potempa, Gary	**MLB**	**6–0**	**234**	**Sr**	**Niles, Ill.**
Pszeracki, Joe	LB	5–11	224	So	Ambridge, Pa.
Quehl, Steve	TE	6–4	238	Jr	Cincinnati, Ohio
Rohan, Andrew	C	6–1	234	Jr	Cincinnati, Ohio
Rudnick, Tim	**RCB**	**5–10**	**187**	**Sr**	**Chicago, Ill.**
Rutkowski, Frank	DT	6–4	241	So	Middletown, Del.
Samuel, Al	HB	6–1	178	Jr	Newport News, Va.
Sarb, Pat	DB	6–0	184	So	Dearborn, Mich.
Sawicz, Paul	T	6–4	231	Sr	Lackawanna, N.Y.
Scales, Ed	LB	6–3	198	Sr	Saginaw, Mich.
Slager, Rick	QB	5–11	185	So	Columbus, Ohio
Smith, Sherman	LB	6–2	210	Jr	Chillicothe, Mo.
Stock, Jim	**DE**	**6–3**	**225**	**So**	**Barberton, Ohio**
Sullivan, Tim	LB	6–3	227	Sr	Des Moines, Iowa
Susko, Larry	DT	6–1	262	Sr	Sharpsville, Pa.
Sweeney, Robert	C	6–5	244	Jr	Salem, Mass.
Sylvester, Steve	**RT**	**6–4**	**248**	**So**	**Milford, Ohio**
Szatko, Greg	DT	6–4	241	Sr	Western Springs, Ill.
Thomas, Robert	K	5–10	178	Sr	Rochester, N.Y.
Townsend, Mike	**FS**	**6–3**	**183**	**Sr**	**Hamilton, Ohio**
Townsend, Willie	SE	6–3	196	Sr	Hamilton, Ohio
Trosko, Fred	QB	6–2	195	So	Ypsilanti, Mich.
Walls, Bob	SE	5–10	160	So	Cohasset, Mass.
Walsh, Robert	LB	6–2	215	So	Maywood, N.J.
Washington, Bob	SE	6–0	173	Sr	Steubenville, Ohio
Wasilevich, Max	T	6–3	242	Sr	Dearborn Heights, Mich.
Webb, Mike	LB	6–2	237	Sr	New Castle, Del.
Weber, Robin	TE	6–5	247	So	Dallas, Texas
Wujciak, Al	G	6–2	230	So	Newark, N.J.
Zanot, Robert	DB	6–0	183	So	Riverton, Ill.
Zloch, James	DB	6–0	180	Sr	Fort Lauderdale, Fla.

1977

11–1–0

(includes 38–10 Cotton Bowl victory over Texas)
Dan Devine, head coach

	Pos	Ht	Wt	Yr	Hometown
Alvarado, Art	FS	6–2	188	Jr	Los Angeles, Calif.
Becker, Doug	**OLB**	**6–0**	**223**	**Sr**	**Hamilton, Ohio**
Boggs, Pat	LB	6–2	221	So	Columbus, Ohio
Bradley, Luther	**CB**	**6–2**	**204**	**Sr**	**Muncie, Ind.**
Browner, Jim	**SS**	**6–3**	**209**	**Jr**	**Warren, Ohio**
Browner, Ross	**DE**	**6–3**	**247**	**Sr**	**Warren, Ohio**
Burgmeier, Ted	**CB**	**5–11**	**186**	**Sr**	**East Dubuque, Ill.**
Bush, Rob	DE	6–6	230	So	Amsterdam, N.Y.
Calhoun, Mike	**DT**	**6–5**	**242**	**Jr**	**Austintown, Ohio**
Case, Jay	DT	6–3	234	Jr	Cincinnati, Ohio
Christensen, Ross	SS	6–1	192	Sr	Racine, Wis.
Crippin, Jeff	C	6–3	225	So	Kansas City, Mo.
Czaja, Mark	TE-DE	6–5	240	So	Lewiston, N.Y.
DeCicco, Nick	CB	5–10	193	Sr	South Bend, Ind.
Dickerson, Tyree	HB	6–2	183	So	Indianapolis, Ind.
Dike, Ken	**DT**	**6–2**	**233**	**Sr**	**Merrillville, Ind.**
Domin, Tom	SE-HB	6–3	204	Jr	Villa Park, Ill.
Dover, Steve	HB	6–1	196	Jr	Kemmerer, Wyo.
Eurick, Terry	HB	5–10	196	Sr	Saginaw, Mich.
Ferguson, Vagas	**HB-FB**	**6–1**	**195**	**So**	**Richmond, Ind.**
Flynn, Tom	CB	6–0	170	Jr	West Palm Beach, Fla.
Foley, Tim	**LT**	**6–5**	**243**	**So**	**Cincinnati, Ohio**
Forystek, Gary	QB	6–2	197	Sr	Livonia, Mich.
Fry, Willie	**DE**	**6–3**	**242**	**Sr**	**Memphis, Tenn.**
Golic, Bob	**MG**	**6–3**	**244**	**Jr**	**Willowick, Ohio**
Gray, Ian	DT	6–6	238	So	New York, N.Y.
Grindinger, Dennis	TE	6–6	224	Jr	Dallas, Texas
Haines, Kris	**SE**	**6–0**	**175**	**Jr**	**Sidney, Ohio**
Harrison, Randy	FS	6–1	207	Jr	Hammond, Ind.
Hart, Kevin	TE	6–4	234	Jr	Birmingham, Mich.
Hart, Speedy	SE	6–1	193	So	Phoenix, Ariz.
Hautman, Jim	C	6–3	238	Jr	Cincinnati, Ohio
Heavens, Jerome	**FB**	**6–0**	**204**	**Jr**	**East St. Louis, Ill.**
Heimkreiter, Steve	**OLB**	**6–2**	**228**	**Jr**	**Cincinnati, Ohio**
Horansky, Ted	**LG**	**6–3**	**244**	**Jr**	**Cleveland Heights, Ohio**
Huffman, Dave	**C**	**6–5**	**241**	**Jr**	**Dallas, Texas**

FIGHTING IRISH MADNESS

	Pos	Ht	Wt	Yr	Hometown
Hufford, Larry	G	6–3	236	So	Trenton, Ohio
Hughes, Ernie	**RG**	**6–3**	**248**	**Sr**	**Boise, Idaho**
Johnson, Pete	LB	6–4	249	Sr	Fond du Lac, Wis.
Johnson, Phil	CB	6–0	196	Jr	Fond du Lac, Wis.
Knott, Dan	HB	6–1	201	Sr	Chowchilla, Calif.
Leon, John	G	6–2	233	So	Wellesburg, W. Va.
Leopold, Leroy	LB	6–2	213	So	Port Arthur, Texas
Lisch, Rusty	QB	6–4	208	Jr	Belleville, Ill.
MacAfee, Ken	**TE**	**6–4**	**250**	**Sr**	**Brockton, Mass.**
Martinovich, Rob	DT	6–5	242	So	Houston, Texas
McCormick, Keith	T	6–5	225	So	Omaha, Neb.
McDaniels, Steve	**RT**	**6–6**	**260**	**Sr**	**Seattle, Wash.**
Merriweather, Ron	FB	6–0	193	So	San Marcos, Texas
Meyer, Howard	G-C	6–3	226	Jr	San Jose, Calif.
Mitchell, David	HB	6–0	190	So	Phoenix, Ariz.
Montana, Joe	**QB**	**6–3**	**191**	**Jr**	**Monongahela, Pa.**
Morse, Jim	CB	6–2	182	Jr	Muskegon, Mich.
Muhlenkamp, Chris	TE-LB	6–3	218	So	Ansonia, Ohio
Muno, Kevin	QB-P	6–0	174	So	Playa del Rey, Calif.
Murphy, Terry	C	6–1	208	Sr	Saginaw, Mich.
Orsini, Steve	FB	5–10	194	Sr	Hummelstown, Pa.
Pallas, Pete	FB	6–2	204	Jr	Yakima, Wash.
Quinn, Mark	C	6–4	224	So	Indianapolis, Ind.
Rachal, Vince	CB	6–2	186	Jr	Houston, Texas
Rayam, Hardy	DT	6–5	243	So	Orlando, Fla.
Reeve, Dave	K	6–3	202	Sr	Bloomington, Ind.
Restic, Joe	**FS-P**	**6–2**	**190**	**Jr**	**Milford, Mass.**
Ryan, K.C.	LB	6–3	222	So	Birmingham, Mich.
Schmitz, Steve	HB	5–11	195	Sr	Lakewood, Ohio
Scully, John	T	6–4	227	So	Huntington, N.Y.
Simon, Tim	SE	5–10	180	Sr	Pontiac, Mich.
Thomas, John	DE	6–4	233	So	Thomasville, N.C.
Thuney, Mark	T	6–2	226	So	Ketterington, Ohio
Tull, Bob	T	6–3	244	Sr	South Bend, Ind.
Unis, Joe	K	5–8	177	So	Dallas, Texas
VanDenburgh, Tom	DE	6–4	228	So	Merrillville, Ind.
Vinson, Dave	G	6–2	237	Sr	Liberty, Texas
Waymer, Dave	**HB-CB**	**6–3**	**186**	**So**	**Charlotte, N.C.**
Weston, Jeff	DT	6–4	258	Jr	Rochester, N.Y.
Whittington, Mike	LB	6–2	219	So	Miami, Fla.
Wroblewski, Tom	G	6–3	233	So	Indianapolis, Ind.
Zettek, Scott	DE-DT	6–5	226	So	Elk Grove Village, Ill.

1988

12–0–0

(includes 34–21 Fiesta Bowl victory over West Virginia)
Lou Holtz, head coach

	Pos	Ht	Wt	Yr	Hometown
Alaniz, Steve	SE	6–2	196	Sr	Edinburg, Texas
Ale, Arnold	LB	6–4	200	Fr	Carson, Calif.
Allen, Joe	T	6–4	268	So	Chicago, Ill.
Alm, Jeff	**DT**	**6–7**	**248**	**Jr**	**Orland Park, Ill.**
Anderson, Shawn	G	6–3	253	Jr	Omaha, Neb.
Balentine, Norm	T	6–5	266	So	Florissant, Mo.
Banks, Braxston	FB	6–3	211	Jr	Hayward, Calif.
Belles, Steve	QB	6–4	211	Sr	Phoenix, Ariz.
Bodine, Jerry	CB	6–0	171	So	Hazen, N.D.
Bolcar, Ned	LB	6–2	232	Sr	Phillipsburg, N.J.
Boyd, Walter	RB	6–0	195	Fr	Hillsborough, N.C.
Brennan, Mike	TE	6–5	246	Sr	Severna Park, Md.
Brooks, Tony	TB	6–2	218	So	Tulsa, Okla.
Brown, Dean	**QT**	**6–3**	**283**	**Jr**	**Canton, Ohio**
Brown, Derek	**TE**	**6–7**	**235**	**Fr**	**Merritt Island, Fla.**
Bufton, Scott	LB	6–0	225	Sr	Catasauqua, Pa.
Callan, Mike	DT	6–4	249	So	Ardmore, Pa.
Connor, Sean	P	6–7	218	Sr	Zeigler, Ill.
Crounse, Michael	DT	6–2	264	Jr	Endicott, N.Y.
Culver, Rodney	RB/DB	6–0	212	Fr	Detroit, Mich.
Dahl, Bob	DT	6–5	248	So	Chagrin Falls, Ohio
Davis, Greg	SS	6–1	198	So	Hollywood, Fla.
Davis, Shawn	WR/DB	6–0	170	Fr	Tulsa, Okla.
deManigold, Marc	DT	6–5	232	Fr	Grosse Point Woods, Mich.
Dillard, James	FL	6–1	180	So	Columbus, Ohio
DiOrio, Doug	FS	5–10	187	Jr	Worthington, Ohio
Dobbins, Marc	SS	6–0	197	Jr	Chicago, Ill.
Earley, Rich	SS	6–0	181	Jr	Lisle, Ill.
Eilers, Pat	FL	5–11	197	Sr	St. Paul, Minn.
Fallon, Patrick	SE	6–0	187	Jr	Pittsfield, Mass.
Farrell, Joe	LB	5–11	214	Jr	Oak Lawn, Ill.
FitzGerald, Ted	DT	6–5	271	Jr	Wayne, N.J.
Flannery, Bryan	DT	6–3	249	Jr	Lakewood, Ohio
Foley, John	DT	6–4	251	Jr	Chicago, Ill.
Francisco, D'Juan	CB	5–11	187	Sr	Cincinnati, Ohio
Gordon, Flash	**DE**	**6–3**	**214**	**Sr**	**Hillside, N.J.**
Gorman, Tom	DT	6–6	255	Sr	Evergreen Park, Ill.
Graham, Kent	QB	6–5	228	So	Wheaton, Ill.
Graham, Pete	QB	6–3	207	Sr	Rumson, N.J.
Green, Mark	**TB**	**6–0**	**184**	**Sr**	**Riverside, Calif.**
Grimm, Donn	LB	6–2	224	So	Scottsdale, Pa.
Grunhard, Tim	**TG**	**6–3**	**279**	**Jr**	**Chicago, Ill.**
Hackett, Billy	K	6–1	184	So	Sarasota, Fla.
Hall, Justin	OL	6–5	290	Fr	Dallas, Texas
Harazin, Mike	C	6–5	232	So	Burbank, Ill.
Hartweger, Pete	P	6–0	178	Sr	Creve Coeur, Md.
Healy, Ted	G	6–4	258	Jr	S. Weymouth, Mass.
Heck, Andy	**TT**	**6–7**	**258**	**Sr**	**Annandale, Va.**

FIGHTING IRISH MADNESS

	Pos	Ht	Wt	Yr	Hometown
Heldt, Mike	C	6–4	258	So	**Tampa, Fla.**
Ho, Reggie	K	5–5	135	Jr	Kaneohe, Hawaii
Ismail, Raghib	SE-RB	5–10	175	Fr	**Wilkes-Barre, Pa.**
Jacobs, Frank	TE	6–5	234	So	Highland Heights, Ky.
Jandric, David	FS	6–2	192	Jr	Omaha, Neb.
Jarosz, Joe	FB	5–11	205	Sr	Arlington Heights, Ill.
Johnson, Anthony	**FB**	**6–0**	**225**	**Jr**	**South Bend, Ind.**
Jones, Andre	DE	6–4	215	So	Hyattsville, Md.
Jurkovic, Mirko	DT	6–5	270	Fr	Calumet City, Ill.
Killian, Chuck	T	6–5	264	Sr	Philadelphia, Pa.
Kinsherf, Jim	C	6–4	252	So	Braintree, Mass.
Knapp, Lindsey	OL	6–6	235	Fr	Deerfield, Ill.
Kowalkowski, Scott	DE	6–2	226	So	Farmington Hills, Mich.
Lark, Antwon	CB	5–11	177	So	Santa Ana, Calif.
Lippincott, Marty	T	6–5	284	Sr	Philadelphia, Pa.
Lyght, Todd	**CB**	**6–1**	**181**	**So**	**Flint, Mich.**
Mannelly, Bernard	DT	6–4	230	Fr	Marietta, Ga.
Marshall, George	DT	6–2	243	So	Somerset, N.J.
McDevitt, Dan	CB	5–10	167	Sr	Chicago, Ill.
McDonald, Devon	DE	6–3	220	Fr	Paterson, N.J.
McGuire, Gene	OL	6–5	265	Fr	Panama City, Fla.
McLoone, Mike	FS	5–11	183	Jr	Dunedin, Fla.
McNamara, Ted	FB	5–11	232	Jr	Dallas, Texas
McShane, Kevin	DE	6–3	219	Jr	Joliet, Ill.
Mihalko, Ryan	FB	6–2	234	So	Pelham, N.H.
Neidell, David	K	5–8	168	So	Tulsa, Okla.
Poorman, George	QB/DB	6–2	185	Fr	Palatine, Ill.
Prinzivalli, Dave	G	6–2	247	Jr	Kaneohe, Hawaii
Pritchett, Wes	**MLB**	**6–6**	**251**	**Sr**	**Atlanta, Ga.**
Rice, Tony	**QB**	**6–1**	**198**	**Jr**	**Woodruff, S.C.**
Ridgley, Troy	LB	6–4	255	Fr	Baden, Pa.
Robb, Aaron	FL	6–1	192	Sr	Coeur d'Alene, Idaho
Roddy, Steve	DT	6–2	237	Sr	Harleysville, Pa.
Rosenberg, David	DE	6–2	204	So	Sarasota, Fla.
Ryan, Tim	**QG**	**6–4**	**245**	**So**	**Kansas City, Mo.**
Sandri, Winston	G	6–4	253	So	Raleigh, N.C.
Satterfield, Bob	CB	6–0	181	Sr	Encino, Calif.
Scruggs, Martin	DB/WR	6–1	165	Fr	Abilene, Texas
Setzer, Rusty	RB/DB	5–9	180	Fr	Gary, Ind.
Sexton, Jim	P	6–0	188	So	South Bend, Ind.
Shannon, Brian	DT	6–5	242	So	New Wilmington, Pa.
Smagala, Stan	**CB**	**5–11**	**186**	**Jr**	**Burbank, Ill.**
Smalls, Michael	LB	6–3	220	Fr	Rialto, Calif.
Smith, Rod	RB	6–1	183	Fr	St. Paul, Minn.
Smith, Tony	WR	6–2	170	Fr	Gary, Ind.
Southall, Corny	FS	6–2	194	Sr	Rochester, N.Y.
Spears, Kenny	RB	6–2	215	Fr	Atlanta, Ga.
Stams, Frank	**DE**	**6–4**	**237**	**Sr**	**Akron, Ohio**
Stonebreaker, Mike	**ELB**	**6–1**	**228**	**Jr**	**River Ridge, La.**
Streeter, George	**SS**	**6–2**	**212**	**Sr**	**Chicago, Ill.**
Terrell, Pat	**FS**	**6–0**	**195**	**Jr**	**St. Petersburg, Fla.**
Watters, Ricky	**FL**	**6–2**	**201**	**So**	**Harrisburg, Pa.**
West, Rod	TE	6–3	234	Jr	New Orleans, La.
Williams, George	**DT**	**6–3**	**282**	**So**	**Willingboro, N.J.**
Wodecki, Darryl	T	6–4	254	So	Chagrin Falls, Ohio
Zackrison, Kurt	DE	6–3	230	Sr	Elmhurst, Ill.
Zorich, Chris	**NT**	**6–1**	**260**	**So**	**Chicago, Ill.**

BIBLIOGRAPHY

Anderson, Heartley William, with Emil Klosinski. *Notre Dame, Chicago Bears, and Hunk: Football Memoirs in Highlight.* Garden City, N.Y.: Doubleday, 1962.

Beach, Jim and Daniel Moore. *Army vs. Notre Dame: The Big Game, 1913–1947.* New York: Random House Inc., 1948.

Celizic, Mike. *The Biggest Game of Them All: Notre Dame, Michigan State, and the Fall of '66.* New York: Simon & Schuster, 1992.

Condon, Dave and Chet Grant, Bob Best. *Notre Dame Football: The Golden Tradition.* South Bend, Ind.: Icarus Press, 1982.

Connor, Jack. *Leahy's Lads: The Story of the Famous Notre Dame Football Teams of the 1940s.* South Bend, Ind.: Diamond Communications Inc., 1994.

Cromartie, Bill and Jody H. Brown. *The Glamor Game: Notre Dame vs. USC.* Nashville, Tenn.: Rutledge Hill Press, 1989.

Danzig, Allison. *Oh, How They Played the Game: The early days of football and the heroes who made it great.* New York: The Macmillan Co., 1971.

Delsohn, Steve. *Talking Irish: The Oral History of Notre Dame Football.* New York: Avon Books Inc., 1998.

Devine, Dan with Michael R. Steele. *Simply Devine: Memoirs of a Hall of Fame Coach.* Champaign, Ill.: Sports Publishing Inc., 2000.

Doyle, Joe and Ross A. Howell, Jr., ed. *Fighting Irish: A Century of Notre Dame Football.* Charlottesville, Va.: Howell Press, 1987.

Faust, Gerry and John Heisler, Bob Logan. *Gerry Faust's Tales from the Notre Dame Sideline.* Champaign, Ill.: Sports Publishing L.L.C., 2004.

Fitzgerald, Ed. *Kick-Off!* New York: Bantam Books Inc., 1948.

Gekas, George. *The Life and Times of George Gipp.* South Bend, Ind.: and books, 1987.

Heisler, John and Mike Enright, eds. *1998 Notre Dame Football Guide.* South Bend, Ind.: University of Notre Dame, Department of Sports Information, 1998.

Holtz, Lou with John Heisler. *The Fighting Spirit: A Championship Season at Notre Dame.* New York: Simon & Schuster Inc., 1989.

Katz, Fred, ed. *The Glory of Notre Dame: 22 Great Stories on Fighting Irish Football from the Pages of* SPORT *Magazine.* Bartholomew House Ltd., 1971.

Krause, Moose and Stephen Singular. *Notre Dame's Greatest Coaches: Rockne, Leahy, Parseghian, Holtz.* New York: Simon & Schuster Inc., 1993.

Kryk, John. *Natural Enemies: The Notre Dame-Michigan Football Feud.* Kansas City, Mo.: Andrews and McMeel, 1994.

Layden, Joe. *Notre Dame Football A-Z.* Dallas, Texas: Taylor Publishing Co., 1997.

Leckie, Robert. *The Story of Football: A lavishly illustrated history of America's exciting gridiron sport.* New York: Random House Inc., 1965.

McCallum, John D. and Paul Castner. *We Remember Rockne.* Huntington, Ind.: Our Sunday Visitor Inc., 1975.

Peterson, James A. *The Four Horsemen of Notre Dame.* Chicago: Hinckley & Schmitt, 1959.

Robinson, Ray. *Rockne of Notre Dame: The Making of a Football Legend.* New York: Oxford University Press, 1999.

Sargent, Jim. "Jerry Groom, All-American: Notre Dame Football, the Chicago Cardinals, and Coach Frank Leahy's Lads." *The Coffin Corner,* Vol. 26, No. 3, 2004: 6.

Schoor, Gene. *100 Years of Notre Dame Football.* New York: William Morrow and Co. Inc., 1987.

Shields, Mike. *"Fight to Win": The Greatest Moments in Notre Dame Football History.* Chicago: Shillelagh Books Inc., 1982.

Sperber, Murray. *Shake Down the Thunder: The Creation of Notre Dame Football.* New York: Henry Holt and Co., 1993.

Walker, Doug and John Heisler, *2005 Notre Dame Football Guide.* Notre Dame, Ind.: University of Notre Dame, Department of Sports Information, 2005.

Wallace, Francis. Notre Dame: From Knute Rockne to Ara Parseghian. New York: David McKay Co. Inc., 1967.

BIBLIOGRAPHY

WEB SITES

Associated Press. "Notre Dame fans want green-letter day for Gipp." ESPN.com. http://sports.espn.go.com/ncf/news/story?id=2190952, Oct. 14, 2005.

Associated Press. "Weis joins Rockne in record books with victory." http://sports.espn.go.com/ncf/recap?confId=&gameId=252530130, Sept. 10, 2005.

Associated Press. "Spartans win fifth straight at Notre Dame." http://sports.espn.go.com/ncf/recap?gameId=2526000 87, Sept. 17, 2005.

Associated Press. "Irish snap home skid, beat BYU behind Quinn's six TDs." http://sports.espn.go.com/ncf/recap?gameId=25295008 7&confId=null, Oct. 22, 2005.

Associated Press. "Quinn tosses three TDs as Irish top reeling Vols." http://sports.espn.go.com/ncf/recap?gameId=2530900 87, Nov. 5, 2005.

Associated Press. "Weis grants little boy's dying wish." http://sports.espn.go.com/ncf/news/story?id=2172623, Sept. 26, 2005.

Associated Press. "Quinn-Stovall connection helps upend Midshipmen." http://sports.espn.go.com/ncf/recap?gameId=2531600 87&confId=null, Nov. 12, 2006.

Associated Press. "Fighting Irish struggle early, pull out win over Syracuse." http://sports.espn.go.com/ncf/recap?gameId=2532300 87&confId=null&date=2005 1119, Nov. 19, 2005.

Associated Press. "Irish hold off Stanford upset bid, become BCS eligible." http://sports.espn.go.com/ncf/recap?gameId=2533000 24, Nov. 26, 2005.

Associated Press. "Smith, Ginn lift speedy Ohio State to another Fiesta title." http://sports.espn.go.com/ncf/recap?gameId=2600201 94, Jan. 2, 2006.

Chval, Craig. "Game Day Magazine catches up with Mr. Fling and Mr. Cling." University of Notre Dame Official Athletic Site. http://und.cstv.com/sports/m-footbl/spec-rel/100104 aae.html, Oct. 1, 2004.

ESPN.com news services. "Notre Dame extends Weis through 2015." http://sports.espn.go.com/ncf/news/story?id=2207478, Oct. 30, 2005.

Forde, Pat. "Weis embraces intangibles only ND can offer."

http://sports.espn.go.com/ espn/columns/story?columnist=forde_pat&id=2131302, Aug. 11, 2005.

Forde, Pat. "Quinn has the tools to survive media hype." http://sports.espn.go.com/ espn/columns/story?columnist=forde_pat&id=2449290 &clpos=spotlight&clid=tab1pos1, May 18, 2006.

Friend, Tom. "Irish eyes attract Clausen to South Bend." *ESPN The Magazine.* http://sports.espn.go.com/ ncaa/recruiting/news/story ?id=2417732, April 22, 2006.

McShay, Todd. "Stanton could challenge Quinn for top spot." *Scouts Inc.* http://insider.espn.go.com /nfl/insider/columns/story ?columnist=mcshay_todd&i d=2438563&action=login&a ppRedirect=http%3a%2f%2 finsider.espn.go.com%2fnfl %2finsider%2fcolumns%2fs tory%3fcolumnist%3dmc-shay_todd%26id%3d243856 3, May 9, 2006.

Moran, Malcolm. "Leinart carries Southern Cal to dramatic defeat of Notre Dame." *USA Today.* http://www.usatoday.com/s ports/college/football/gam es/2005–10–15-usc-notre-dame_x.htm, Oct. 15, 2006.

University of Notre Dame Official Athletic Site. "Former Notre Dame Football All-American Bob Dove Dies at the Age of 85." http://und.cstv.com/sports /monogramclub/spec-rel/ 042106aad.html, April 21, 2006.

University of Notre Dame Official Athletic Site. "George Kunz Profile." http://und.cstv.com/sports /m-footbl/mtt/kunz_george 00.html.

Wikipedia. "George Kunz." http://en.wikipedia.org/wiki /George_Kunz, April 7, 2006.

Wojciechowski, Gene. "Irish come out swinging for Weis' debut." ESPN.com. http://proxy.espn.go.com/ espn/columns/story?columnist=wojciechowski_gene&id =2151291, Sept. 4, 2005.

Wojciechowski, Gene. "USC-ND thriller destined to be remembered." ESPN.com. http://sports.espn.go.com/ espn/columns/story?columnist=wojciechowski_gene&id =2192737, Oct. 15, 2005.

INDEX

Printed in the USA
CPSIA information can be obtained
at www.ICGtesting.com
JSHW012049140824
68134JS00035B/3332